RUG

How to Move
What You're Tripping Over
and Lead with H.E.A.R.T.

Sherry Whitaker Budziak
and Kevin G. Ordoñez

Paperback ISBN: 978-1-963732-23-8
Hardback ISBN: 978-1-963732-24-5

Published by

The Publishing Pad
www.thepublishingpad.com

What Leaders Say About *RUG*

66 *RUG* is a wake-up call for every leader who's been tripping over what they don't see. Sherry and Kevin have written a guide that's both deeply human and immediately useful. They remind us that leadership isn't about pretending we have it all figured out—it's about having the courage to lift the rug, face what's underneath, and move forward with empathy and purpose.

—Heather Monahan, Top 50 Keynote Speaker, Best Selling Author of *Confidence Creator*, Podcast Host

66 All leaders and teams struggle to see their blind spots and remedy them. Sherry's concept of identifying the *RUGs* that trip us up and using her H.E.A.R.T. method to optimize operational excellence provides a fresh, engaging, and non-threatening way to increase productivity, engagement, and growth. If you only read 3 books this year, make *RUG* one of them!

—Tim Shurr, Leadership and Unconscious Bias Expert, Bestselling Author of *One Belief Away*

66 If you lead a team or a company, you need to read this book. This book will give you the courage and the words to lead with true emotion and trust. This book is a reminder that our organizations are not a set of processes, but made up of people who want to be heard, challenged, and trusted. One lesson stands out for me: Empowerment is the oxygen of innovation. I have found this to be true at my organization. When I give my staff the tools and training, and then empower them to create great things, they do it willingly and with pride. Hold a book club at your company and read this book together.

—Joanna M. Pineda, CEO and Chief Troublemaker, Matrix Group International, Inc.

66 *RUG* pulls no punches. It invites leaders to lift what's been swept beneath the surface and face it with courage, curiosity, and heart. It's a manual for transformation that proves small moves create big ripples when you're brave enough to move what's in your way.

— Judi Holler, USA Today Bestselling Author of *Holler at Your Dreams*

66 *RUG* provides solid footing to support leaders as they navigate uncertain pathways to achieve transformation in the face of disruption. Sherry and Kevin create a space for clarity, empathy and success.

—Gary A LaBranche, FASAE, CAE, Chief Executive Officer, RIMS, The Risk Management Society

66 *RUG* is a compelling and practical guide to authentic leadership. Sherry and Kevin blend wisdom, vulnerability, and experience to show how leading with H.E.A.R.T. (Humanize, Empower, Ascend, Reimagine, Transform) creates meaningful impact and real organizational change. Their stories remind leaders that growth begins with courage and self-awareness. Every page offers insight for those seeking to build stronger teams, more compassionate workplaces, and more purposeful leadership journeys.

—Donald Dea, Board Chair, America's VetDogs & Guide Dog Foundation, President & Cofounder, Shark Innovations Corporation

66 *RUG* met me where I lead—at the intersection of purpose and possibility. Sherry and Kevin give language and tools to a style I've practiced for years, and their H.E.A.R.T. framework—humanize, empower, ascend, reimagine, transform—makes courageous leadership usable by anyone at any level. The affirmations resonate, the stories stick, and the reminder that "you don't need a title to move the rug" is pure fuel. This isn't theory; it's a practical playbook for building cultures where people feel seen, trusted, and energized to act. If you're turning around systems or elevating teams, start here. Read it, share it, and move something.

—Artesha Moore, FASAE, CAE, President & CEO of Association Forum

Authors' Note

For years, through our consulting work, we've helped leaders and teams uncover what was holding them back—the "rugs" they kept tripping over. Together, we have guided organizations to name their challenges, face them with courage, and move forward stronger than before. But when disruption hit our own lives, we realized these lessons weren't just professional. They were deeply personal.

This book was born from that understanding. The same principles that help organizations reimagine and transform also help people heal, rebuild, and rise. *RUG* is both a roadmap and a reflection—of what we have seen in boardrooms and what we have lived ourselves. Our hope is that these stories inspire you to move your own rug, lead with H.E.A.R.T., and discover what transformation looks like on the other side of disruption.

Dedication

For my daughters,
who gave me a reason to rise,
even when the world stood still.

For my parents,
Thank you for teaching me to be strong and
for always believing I could move the rug.

And for everyone who has ever tripped, fallen,
gotten back up, and moved forward—
you are not alone.

Sherry

Dedication

For Taryn and Justin,
who remind me daily that love is the truest measure
of a life well lived.

For my parents,
who gave me every opportunity to grow
and taught me the power of leading with all your heart.
Though they are gone,
their lessons remain the foundation beneath my steps.

And for everyone learning to give fully,
to rise after loss,
and to keep moving forward —
your heart will always show the way.

Kevin

Acknowledgment

This book would not exist without the incredible people who supported, inspired, and believed in me through every step of this journey.

To **my daughters**—thank you for grounding me in purpose and reminding me daily of what true resilience looks like. Your love is my greatest gift.

To **my parents**—your unwavering strength and encouragement gave me the courage to keep going when it felt impossible. This book carries your spirit on every page.

To **Kevin Ordoñez**—my longtime business partner and co-creator of the H.E.A.R.T. Powered Leadership™ framework. Thank you for walking beside me through every challenge and every triumph. Your insight, collaboration, and friendship have made this work richer than I ever could have imagined.

To the **.orgSource Team**—your passion, creativity, commitment to our customers and H.E.A.R.T. inspire me daily. Thank you for bringing our shared vision to life with integrity and excellence.

To **our clients and partners**—thank you for trusting us to guide you through pivotal moments of change. Your courage to move your own rugs has fueled the lessons in this book.

To **Tim Shurr, MA**—your "One Belief Away" method changed the trajectory of my life. You helped me uncover the hidden beliefs that kept me stuck and showed me how to rewrite my story. Your wisdom shaped not only my healing but the very heart of this book and helped me move the *RUG*. I am forever grateful!

To **Judi Holler**—thank you for helping me find my voice again when I needed it most.

To **my dear friends and mentors**—thank you for your support, encouragement, and belief when I needed it most. You know who you are.

And finally, to **you, the reader**—thank you for picking up this book. May it give you the clarity, courage, and companionship you need to move your own rug and lead with H.E.A.R.T.

With deepest gratitude,
Sherry

Table of Contents

About the Authors

Sherry Whitaker Budziak is a visionary leader in organizational and digital strategy. As an entrepreneur and Founder and CEO of .orgSource, Sherry has helped guide hundreds of associations and nonprofits through growth, disruption, and the rapidly changing landscape of technology. Her expertise bridges the gap between strategy and humanity, offering practical pathways for leaders who want to stay relevant, resilient, and human in the digital age.

Sherry's leadership is grounded in decades of experience and forged by personal transformation. Following the sudden loss of her husband, she channeled her grief into growth and co-created the H.E.A.R.T.

Powered Leadership™ framework to help others lead through adversity and challenging times. A top keynote speaker and podcast host, she is known for blending strategic insight with empathy, candor, and humor. Sherry is passionate about empowering people to reimagine what's possible—especially when the world turns upside down.

Kevin G. Ordoñez is the President and Managing Director of .orgSource and has partnered with Sherry for more than 20 years to help leaders modernize their organizations and embrace digital innovation, a nationally recognized thought leader in digital transformation, technology strategy, and association governance. He brings decades of experience helping mission-driven organizations align leadership, culture, and systems to accelerate innovation and sustainable growth with deep expertise in technology strategy, governance, and executive alignment. Kevin has led hundreds of successful client engagements.

Together, Sherry and Kevin bring a rare combination of practical experience, strategic insight, and compassionate, human-centered leadership. As highly sought-after speakers, consultants, and trusted collaborators, they've guided hundreds of organizations through transformation across nonprofit, healthcare, and professional services sectors. Their work is reshaping leadership conversations, creating a more forward-thinking, resilient, and people-focused future across industries.

Sherry and Kevin are the authors of Association 4.0®—an Entrepreneurial Approach to Risk, Courage and Transformation and Association 4.0®—Positioning for Success in an Era of Disruption.

How to Use This Book

This book is more than a story. It's a toolkit for transformation.

Whether you're leading a company, a team, a classroom, or simply leading yourself through disruption, you'll find something in these pages to guide, challenge, and support you. This book is designed to be read cover to cover, but it's also built so you can return to any chapter when you need a specific kind of wisdom or strength.

Each chapter centers on one pillar of the H.E.A.R.T. Powered Leadership™ framework:

- Humanize – Lead with empathy. Put people first.
- Empower – Trust deeply. Let others lead.
- Ascend – Rise above comfort. Choose growth.
- Reimagine – Challenge norms. See possibility.
- Transform – Rewrite your story. Lead from experience.

For each pillar, we include:
- Stories from our personal and professional lives that bring the principles to life.
- "Kevin's Takes" offer an additional lens on the themes explored in each chapter.
- Rug Reflections to prompt personal insight and self-assessment.
- The Practice – A hands-on exercise to apply the lesson in real time.
- Micro-Moves – Small, powerful actions you can take today.

You can read this book solo or use it with your team. Many organizations have used the H.E.A.R.T. method as a guide for:
- Staff retreats
- Leadership development programs
- Coaching sessions
- Peer mentoring circles

Every chapter has a placeholder for your own notes and reflections. We also offer a downloadable companion journal and training workshops to deepen your journey. Visit rugthebook.com.

However you choose to use this book, come back to it often. Reread the stories. Reflect on your growth. Mark the places where you moved the rug. Because leading with H.E.A.R.T. and moving the *RUG* is not just a one-time insight—it's a lifelong practice.

Welcome to the movement. #MovetheRug

Foreword

Leadership has always fascinated me—not just as a role or title, but as a test of who we are when things break, shift, and demand something new from us. Over the course of my career, I've worked with hundreds of organizations and leaders navigating change and sometimes disruption. But nothing prepared me for the day I witnessed one of the most profound transformations up close—when my business partner and friend, Sherry Whitaker Budziak, was met with a disruption and trauma that changed everything.

I've stood beside Sherry through countless boardrooms, bold initiatives, and complicated client engagements. We've built strategies, solved problems, and helped associations rethink their identity in a world that won't stop changing. However, the strength she demonstrated in the wake of personal tragedy—the clarity, courage, and grace—was a different kind of leadership. It was human. It was healing. It was H.E.A.R.T.

This book reflects everything we've learned, taught, and lived. But more than that, it's a message to anyone who finds themselves facing the unknown, wondering if they have what it takes to rise. I can tell you from experience: Sherry doesn't just rise—she lifts others with her.

RUG isn't a typical leadership book. It doesn't sell formulas or rely on jargon. It invites you into a journey—a deeply personal one, yes—but also a universal one. It offers a framework built from lived experience, forged in adversity, and refined in the work we've done with leaders who dared to move the rug and do things differently.

If you're looking for inspiration, you'll find it here. If you're looking for practical tools, they're here too. But most importantly, if you're looking for permission to lead with empathy, courage, imagination, and resilience, you've come to the right place.

I'm honored to share this book with you, and even more honored to have walked this path with Sherry. What you're about to read is the story of a woman who redefined what it means to lead—and a guide for all of us to do the same.

—Kevin G. Ordoñez
President & Managing Director, .orgSource

Introduction

Disruption rarely arrives with a warning, but when it does, it rips away the familiar and invites us to uncover the hidden obstacles, starting with the rug beneath our feet.

This book is for anyone who has ever hit the floor and thought, *"Now what?"*

Whether you're leading a company, a team, or simply yourself through disruption, I wrote this book to show there is always a way forward—and it begins by moving the rug we're tripping over.

On Dec. 31, 2022, I walked into my bedroom and found my husband, Steve—my partner in every sense of the word—unconscious, lying on the floor beside the bed.

There was no warning. No final words. Just silence.

In that instant, everything I believed to be steady collapsed. The rug wasn't just under him—it was pulled from under my entire life.

If you've ever experienced something like that—something that unravels your world—you know the silence that follows. It's not peaceful. It's deafening. It fills every space. It hollows out your voice. And for a time, it convinces you that the version of yourself you once knew is lost forever.

I've spent most of my life leading people through change. I've helped associations, entrepreneurs, and teams of all sizes adapt to disruption. I've navigated digital transformation, culture clashes, executive resistance, failed systems, fear of AI—you name it. Together with my longtime business partner, Kevin Ordoñez, .orgSource's President and Managing Director and the extraordinary .orgSource consulting team, we've helped hundreds of organizations stand at the edge of what once felt impossible and take the next step forward. Our work spans industries, technologies, and leadership styles, but one belief has always guided us: disruption, while uncomfortable, is the doorway to transformation. It's not something to fear, it's something to work through, learn from, and ultimately grow because of.

But that day…

That day was different.

That was the day I learned that there are some disruptions no roadmap can prepare you for.

In the weeks that followed, everything in me wanted to disappear. To check out. To shut the door and the emails and the Zoom calls and just exist in a quiet grief that didn't ask anything of me.

But I had two daughters watching. I had a business with clients who needed my leadership. I had a life that still had more story left in it—even if I couldn't see it yet.

And I had a decision to make. This book is about that decision.

It's not just about my personal loss. It's about the journey back to myself, and what I discovered along the way about the true nature of leadership.

For most of my career, I believed disruption meant technology, change, or unexpected challenges. But this was personal. This was the kind of disruption that reaches into your identity, unsettles your soul, and rewrites everything you thought you knew about yourself.

And it was in that space, where I was raw, cracked open, and uncertain, that a new kind of clarity emerged.

Together, Kevin and I began to look back at everything we'd learned over the decades: every tough boardroom, every failed rollout we were brought in to fix, every brave leader who dared to try something new.

We started seeing the patterns—not in their spreadsheets, but in their strength. And we realized that leading through disruption wasn't about having all the answers.

It was about leading with H.E.A.R.T. (Humanize, Empower, Ascend, Reimagine, and Transform).

I didn't plan to create a new framework. But life doesn't always wait for your permission to begin again. A week before my birthday—February 14th, Valentine's Day—Kevin and I sat down to reflect on everything we'd seen, learned, and lived through.

That conversation sparked something. It wasn't just a strategy. It wasn't just survival. It was something deeper.

We call it H.E.A.R.T. Powered Leadership™. And while the name might have been inspired by the date, the meaning ran much deeper.

H.E.A.R.T. stands for:
- Humanize – Lead with empathy. Put people first.
- Empower – Trust deeply. Let others lead.
- Ascend – Rise above comfort. Choose growth.
- Reimagine – Challenge norms. See possibility.
- Transform – Rewrite your story. Lead from experience.

We didn't invent these principles. We lived them. Kevin and I had been teaching these ideas in fragments for years, through consulting, speaking, and strategy. But after my personal loss, something shifted. The pieces came together. And for the first time, I saw clearly what had always been guiding us.

This book is both deeply personal and widely applicable. Whether you are leading a team, a company, an association—or simply leading yourself through transition—it's meant to remind you that:
- You are more resilient than you realize.
- You are not alone in the transformation.
- And you are always just one belief, one choice, one move away from becoming the next version of yourself.

A Note on Voice and Collaboration

For simplicity and intimacy, this book is written in my voice—Sherry's—with stories, reflections, and insights gathered over decades of shared experience with Kevin. While I am the storyteller, Kevin's fingerprints are on every page: in the philosophy, the frameworks, and the transformation journeys we've led together across hundreds of associations and organizations.

Together, we wrote this book to explore what it means to be a truly resilient leader in an era defined by rapid digital disruption and personal upheaval. This is our attempt to name what's often left unsaid in leadership: the human side of transformation, the emotional toll of change, and the practical ways to rise stronger together.

Kevin will join us throughout the book, sharing thoughts and stories that reflect his perspective and our shared learning. You'll also find tools, prompts, and micro-actions designed to help you rebuild—not just your organization, but your outlook, your courage, your identity. This book isn't just for those navigating technology or running a business. It's for anyone who tries to lead when the old rules no longer apply.

We wrote this on the other side of loss. But more importantly, we wrote it on the edge of something new. Because while disruption may take things from us, it also gives us a choice. You're holding that choice in your hands right now.

Let's begin.

Prologue

We often think of leadership in terms of performance.

We polish our presence. We perfect our pitches. We lead meetings. We set the strategy.

But real leadership—the kind that changes cultures and transforms lives—starts somewhere far less polished. It begins in the moments we never planned for. The interruptions. The unraveling. The quiet collapse of everything we thought we could control.

For me, that moment came on a winter day I will never forget. It didn't begin in front of an audience or inside a meeting. It began in a room filled with silence—and a rug.

That rug—ordinary, familiar, unnoticed—became more than just a carpet underfoot. It became a mirror. A symbol of everything I had been walking across for years.

Grief tore through my life like a storm. I didn't know how afraid I was of it until it arrived. It broke the shell of certainty I'd built around myself and revealed a truth at the center of every transformation:

We don't lead through heroics. We lead through H.E.A.R.T.

Only after living through loss did I begin to recognize patterns. First in my own life, then in the organizations we have served.

Just as I walked across my own emotional rug, pretending not to notice the frayed edges, I watched teams do the same. They stepped over broken processes, silent suffering, and cultural fatigue—and called it professionalism.

What we refuse to acknowledge, we eventually trip over.

That's why we begin here—with *Humanize*. Not because it's soft, but because it's structural. Foundational. It's where every meaningful transformation begins.

To lead with H.E.A.R.T., we must begin with sight—the courage to see the human behind the title, the emotion behind the data, the story behind the performance. Because we can't move what we won't acknowledge.

This isn't just the story of one woman's loss.

It's an invitation to reexamine the rugs we've all been walking on—and to lead with empathy, presence, and truth.

Chapter 1:
Humanize – The Rug Beneath Our Feet

H.E.A.R.T. Focus:
Humanize – Lead with empathy. Put people first.

The Rug We Didn't See

In a world reshaped by sudden loss, layoffs, and burnout, we've all been forced to confront rugs we didn't realize we were tripping over.

The rug we trip over most is the one we no longer see.

Leadership begins not with strategy, but with sight. It starts with the courage to see beyond the surface—the human behind the title, the emotion behind the data, the story behind the performance. Because we can't move what we refuse to acknowledge.

And sometimes, what we need to acknowledge isn't waiting for us in a boardroom. Sometimes, it's quietly lying beneath our feet, unnoticed until we trip over it.

For me, leadership became intensely personal on one dreadful New Year's Eve day, when I found my husband, Steve—my partner, the father of our children—gone. No warning. No final words. Just silence.

The rug beneath him became more than just carpet. It became a symbol—the rug of invisible survival I'd unknowingly walked across my entire life. Because I realized my grief didn't begin there, on that bedroom floor that day. It had been woven long before.

I had been weaving rugs of survival for years, layered with early losses I never fully processed. At 15, I lost my friend Anthony in a car accident. Then came the heartache of losing my best friend, Michael. Years later, life hit again. Within months, I lost my cousin Greg to leukemia, and both my maternal grandparents.

Each time, I put on an armor. I kept going. I internalized a dangerous belief: that to be strong, I had to remain standing while others fell. That belief became the first thread in the rug I would later trip over.

When Michael died, the school counselor pulled me aside and asked me to look after Michael's girlfriend. They worried she might try to harm herself. I was 17, grieving, and hollowed out, but still, I put on the armor. I became the one who held it all together.

> **Strength isn't standing tall.**
> **It's knowing when to sit with pain.**

That day planted something deep in me: the idea that when things fall apart, I had to be the one left standing. It would take years to untangle that belief.

I cried for Michael privately, carrying questions like bricks in my backpack: *Why did he leave? Why didn't I see it coming? What more could I have done?*

But I did what I'd always done. I moved forward, stayed busy, kept appearing "strong." Over time, without even realizing it, I quietly stitched together my survival, thread by invisible thread. I made a silent agreement with myself: *If I just keep moving, I'll be okay.*

What I didn't see was that I was weaving a rug beneath my own feet—a rug I'd walk across daily, ignoring its frayed edges, until I buckled on top of it.

Nothing prepares you for the disruption that hits your home.

When Steve passed away, I thought I knew how to survive grief. I had done it before—more times than anyone should have to. I believed I had mastered it. That I had proven I could endure the unendurable. And now, I felt I had to do it again for myself, for my daughters, and for everyone watching.

People would ask my mother how I was holding up. She'd respond, "She's fine. She doesn't have a choice. She has two kids to raise, a business to run, and a roof to keep over their heads."

For a while, I believed that too. I even fooled myself. But then came a moment when I couldn't pretend any longer. That's when I learned the truth I'd been outrunning for years: being "the strong one" wasn't true resilience. It was a performance—the armor I'd perfected, hiding all the pain behind it.

Only when I finally allowed myself to sit down—emotionally, spiritually, physically—did I begin to understand what healing truly looks like.

True resilience doesn't come from bypassing pain. It comes from naming it, from sitting with it, from recognizing the patterns we've woven so tightly beneath us, from refusing to trip over the same rug forever just because it's familiar.

> **Real resilience begins where performance ends.**

I rebuilt myself—piece by piece. And in that process, I discovered that the way we lead ourselves through disruption is exactly how we'll lead others through change. Here's what we often overlook: Humanizing leadership is not how we treat others. It starts with how we treat ourselves.

For months, I kept moving. I held everything together for my kids, showed up for everyone else, and told myself I had no choice. But ignoring grief doesn't make it disappear. Instead, burnout moves in with grief. The spark was gone. The joy was gone. And it showed up in my leadership.

The shift came when I admitted I could not do it alone. I joined a women's church group where I saw that vulnerability meant strength. I found a coach and a mental health expert to help me face the limiting beliefs holding me back. Life kept throwing challenges, an unending storm, but seeking help gave me the tools to stand again.

That season taught me something I'll never forget: If we keep pouring out without filling back up, if we bury grief instead of facing it, the cost isn't only personal—it ripples into how we lead, connect, and inspire.

Once I understood this, I began seeing rugs everywhere—in my life and in the organizations I served.

The Rug We Normalize

The inspiration behind the *RUG* started about 10 years ago, during a client meeting in their office conference room. Outside that room, in the hallway just before the threshold, lay an ugly rug—faded, stained, frayed along the edges. Worse yet, it was a hazard. People tripped over it constantly, almost unconsciously lifting their feet higher in that spot, like dancers in a poorly choreographed routine.

At first, I went about my day without saying anything. Then a few days later, I finally asked, "Why don't we just move this rug?"

A staff member paused, as if the question had never occurred to anyone. "We'd need to ask the CEO."

Let that sink in. No one liked the rug. It posed an actual risk. Yet it remained, because of the default belief that we needed permission to move it.

That rug wasn't just worn-out fabric. It was a metaphor for every outdated process, pointless report, redundant meeting, unspoken rule, and cultural quirk that remained simply because "that's how we've always done it."

It represented the invisible friction in our workflows—the trip hazards no one questions because challenging them might mean confronting authority, facing resistance, or disturbing the comfort of routine.

But even more deeply, it represented a culture where people had learned to stop seeing, stop asking, stop caring. They did this not from malice but from weariness.

When we stop questioning systems, we stop seeing the people inside them.

One afternoon, I decided enough was enough. I picked up that rug, rolled it up, and walked down the hallway. As I tucked it into the supply closet, I looked around. Nobody was paying attention. No one noticed. No one asked about it. No one missed it.

But I'll never forget it. In that quiet act, I realized something deeper than I could have imagined: sometimes transformation begins not with a strategy, but with the courage to move the rug.

And sometimes, humanizing a workplace starts by reminding people: You matter enough to stop tripping over the same thing every day.

> **You don't need a title to move the rug.**
> **You need the courage to see it.**

That simple decision became symbolic for me. Since then, I've recognized nearly every organization has its own version of that metaphorical rug. These rugs are inefficiencies that go unquestioned, habits that drain momentum, and silent obstacles tripping up progress.

More importantly, the rug symbolizes fatigue, disengagement, and learned helplessness.

Unless we lead with empathy, unless we ask why the rug is still there and how it affects the people walking across it every day, we'll never change anything that matters.

Humanizing is not just about caring more—it's about seeing what people have stopped saying out loud.

In nearly every transformation project we've led, we've found rugs like that. These are:

- Systems no one trusts.
- Meetings no one needs.
- Traditions with purpose no one remembers.

Yet these rugs shape the way we work. We walk over them daily. And we wonder why we keep tripping.

Kevin's Take: What We Can't See, We Can't Solve

In nearly every transformation project I've been part of, the real issue isn't the strategy—it's the silence. It's the assumptions we don't question, the systems we stop seeing, and the pain we normalize in the name of professionalism. That's why I always say: "If you want to create real change, start by listening for what isn't being said."

—Kevin G. Ordoñez

Seeing the Whole Picture

Digital transformation projects have taught me that behind every system is a story. Behind every key performance indicator is a person. Behind every dashboard is a dream.

One of my earliest professional wins came long before "digital transformation" had a name. It was 1994. Practically no one had a website, especially not a medical association. Email was just beginning to show up on desktops. Most organizations still relied on fax machines and printed manuals.

Yet there we were, proposing something almost no one had seen before: a full online presence for a national medical society that would include the entire National Library of Medicine content in a searchable database, a CPT coding decision-tree tool long before interactive UX was standard, and—because we wanted it to feel cutting-edge—a home-page featuring a spinning brain. For the time, this wasn't incremental progress. It was moonshot thinking.

We weren't just creating an online brochure. We were building an early digital ecosystem—a place where neurosurgeons could access knowledge, explore coding pathways, and experience a new kind of professional identity in a digital space.

When we finally presented the prototype to the website chair, we were proud. The tech felt bold. The vision felt radical. The spinning brain felt clever. Everything in the room signaled excitement until we reached the homepage.

A chair leaned forward and said, calmly and without judgment, "We don't just treat the brain. We treat the spine and the entire central nervous system."

One sentence. Clear. Precise. Human.

In that moment, everything shifted. He wasn't critiquing the animation. He was protecting the truth of who they were. He wanted the digital presence to honor the full scope of their mission, not just the part that made for an eye-catching graphic.

Innovation fails when it flattens identity.

We went back to the drawing board, not to play it safe, but to make it whole. We re-designed navigation centered around Rodin's *The Thinker*—a timeless, human symbol of deep contemplation and the full central nervous system. It grounded the site in accuracy, dignity, and meaning.

Looking back, I see that moment differently. It wasn't about a website at all. It was about leadership. About listening. About remembering that even in the most technical projects, people aren't asking for perfection. They're asking to be understood.

In our rush to automate, streamline, and build what's next, we can forget the people inside the systems. That volunteer member wasn't re-acting to a graphic. He was asking us to see them—to see the fullness of their work, their identity, and their purpose.

That's where humanizing begins. Not with the flash of innovation, but with the humility to ask:

> **What part of someone's story
> am I missing in my rush to innovate?**

That single sentence—*"We treat the entire central nervous system"*—has stayed with me ever since. It reshaped how I approached every project that followed. Because the greatest digital transformations don't just improve systems. They deepen understanding. They strengthen relationships. They make people feel seen.

And that is the heart of Humanize.

The Problem With
Process-First Leadership

We love our frameworks. We love our metrics. We love the comfort of a clean dashboard and the illusion that if the numbers look good, the people must be good too. But transformation doesn't start with software. It starts with sight. You can't transform what you haven't taken the time to humanize.

I've worked with organizations that had world-class technology but broken cultures. Teams exhausted behind immaculate dashboards, emotions buried beneath efficiency, people treated more like extensions of systems than the reason those systems exist in the first place. These were rugs everyone kept tripping over—disconnection masquerading as productivity, disengagement hidden under polished reports, dehumanization packaged as optimization.

You can't innovate if your people feel invisible.

You can't solve a problem you haven't examined.

You can't lead if you're only looking at the surface.

> **Before you redesign anything, ask: What's the real problem beneath the rug?**

Every successful transformation begins with one simple question: *Do we truly understand the problem we're trying to solve?* Not the symptoms. Not the noise. The real problem. The human problem.

Because the best technology strategies don't start with systems.

They start with sight.

The Rug, Reimagined

You may not realize it yet, but there's a rug beneath your feet. Maybe it's woven from stories you no longer tell. From questions you stopped asking. From systems you've learned to walk across without noticing. It might be emotional. It might be cultural. It might be embedded in how your team shows up every day. And it might be holding you—and the people you lead—back.

The truth is that most transformations don't fail because we lack tools or strategy. They fail because we overlook what's right in front of us:

- The unspoken tension.
- The unchallenged tradition.
- The human story we've stopped seeing.

Real change doesn't begin with disruption. It begins with awareness. With empathy. With heart. It begins the moment we pause, look down, and say:

"I see it now. And I'm willing to move it."

That's how we humanize. That's how we lead. That's how we change everything.

Humanizing Your Leadership in Practice

Humanizing isn't soft. It's precise. It's the discipline of leading with clarity about the people behind the process. Here's what that looks like when you're leading yourself and leading your team.

For Leading Yourself:
Slow down enough to actually see the rug you're standing on.

Ask what belief is driving your reaction, not just what task is driving your day.

Pause before solving. Listen before responding. Let the human truth reveal the real problem.

For Leading Your Team:
Make space for the story before the solution.

Ask people what they're experiencing, not just what they're producing.

Treat every system change as a people change first.

> **Humanize first—everything else becomes clearer after that.**

Rug Reflection:
The Rug of Invisible Survival

This rug hides the truth we must acknowledge to humanize our leadership fully.

Use the following prompts to journal in the space provided:

- **What invisible rug are you walking on that blocks your ability to humanize others?**

_____

_____

_____

- **Where are you asking others to trip silently, because "that's how it's always been?"**

_____

_____

_____

- **What part of your own story needs to be acknowledged so you can lead more authentically?**

_____

_____

_____

The Practice:
Humanizing Through Empathy

Apply what you're learning.

Create personas of your team and your customers. Ask:

- **What do they fear?**

_____

_____

_____

- **What motivates them?**

_____

_____

_____

- **Where do they feel unseen?**

_____

_____

_____

Use these insights to inform your next meeting, strategy session, or decision.

The Practice:
Humanizing Yourself

Before you can humanize a team, you have to humanize the person you bring to the room every day. Self-leadership begins with empathy for your own story, your own limits, and your own unspoken needs. This practice helps you slow down enough to see yourself clearly—without judgment, without performance, without the pressure to be "the strong one."

Use these questions as a mirror. Answer them honestly. They will show you where your own rug is, and where you might be asking yourself to trip in silence.

Questions for Self-Leadership

- **What am I carrying into my work today that I haven't acknowledged?**
  Fatigue, worry, grief, pressure—empathy begins by naming what's already inside you.

_____

_____

_____

- **Where am I being hard on myself in ways I would never be with someone I lead?**
  Humanizing yourself means extending the same grace you extend to others.

- **What belief is driving the way I'm showing up right now?**
  Is it a belief rooted in truth... or in fear, habit, or old expectations?

- **What part of my story have I been rushing past or minimizing?**
  You can't lead from a place you refuse to see.

- **Where am I pushing for output instead of caring for my wellbeing?**
  Empathy isn't indulgence. It's maintenance for the long game.

  _____

  _____

  _____

- **What do I actually need today—clarity, rest, connection, boundaries, courage?**
  Most leaders never stop long enough to ask this. Start here.

  _____

  _____

  _____

- **What rug am I still stepping over in my personal leadership?**
  A resentment? A fear? A pattern? A pressure to perform strength instead of practicing it?

  _____

  _____

  _____

Micro-Moves:
Humanize Yourself And Others

Humanizing begins with small shifts—quiet choices that restore connection to yourself and the people you lead. These micro-moves create space for clarity, empathy, and truth to surface, often in the moments we rush past.

- **Cancel an unnecessary meeting.**
  Clearing space is an act of respect for everyone's energy, including your own.

- **Ask someone how they really are—and stay long enough to hear the real answer.**
  Listening is the simplest form of humanizing a workplace.

- **Name what you're feeling before you respond.**
  Self-awareness prevents unnecessary friction and sets a clearer tone for others.

- **Call out a norm that no longer serves your team.**
  Patterns persist until someone is brave enough to say, "This isn't working anymore."

- **Set one boundary today.**
  End on time. Say no kindly. Protect an hour for focused work or rest. Boundaries humanize the leader and the team.

- **Offer yourself the grace you offer others.**
  Ask: "Would I expect someone else to handle this perfectly?" If not, adjust your own expectations.

- **Celebrate a small win—yours or someone else's.**
  Recognition expands what people believe they're capable of, including you.

- **Slow one thing down.**
  A slower moment interrupts the stress pattern, allowing you to lead with presence rather than urgency.

- **Check in with your body.**
  Release the tension you don't notice you're carrying. Your team can feel the difference.

- **Make one intention visible.**
  Before your next conversation, choose how you want to show up—curious, calm, clear—and lead from that place.

These aren't grand gestures. They are micro-adjustments that restore humanity where work often strips it away. When you practice them consistently, you create cultures where people feel seen—starting with you.

The Strength in Seeing

The rug beneath our feet may have gone unnoticed for years—until it caused us to stumble. That stumble didn't break us. It only revealed something essential: our capacity to pause, to question, and to begin again with empathy. The strength wasn't in standing tall—it was in choosing to finally see. Leadership begins with what you choose to see.

Once you begin to humanize the journey, the next step is learning to rise.

That's how you *Humanize* with H.E.A.R.T.

H.E.A.R.T. Summary: HUMANIZE

- See people, not roles.
- Acknowledge invisible struggles.
- Lead with empathy, not just efficiency.

Chapter 2:

Empower – The Rug We Won't Let Go

"When you empower people, you're not just giving
them responsibility; you're giving them the confidence
to rise to the occasion."
—SHERYL SANDBERG

H.E.A.R.T. Focus:
Empower – Trust deeply. Let others lead.

The Rug We Won't Let Go Of

> **Empowerment isn't assigning tasks.
> It's transferring belief.**

Empowerment isn't about giving people to-do lists—it's about creating the kind of culture where people have the courage to move their own rugs. Before I ever led a team or launched a company, I faced a moment that tested my courage and changed the course of my career.

One of the most defining moments of my early career came wrapped in a question I wasn't prepared to ask—and a response that changed everything.

I had just been hired by an association to start and build a for-profit website company. They had the concept, but no roadmap, no team, and no infrastructure. It was up to me to get it off the ground.

It was bold, uncharted, risky, even. It made me worry, too, that I might have made a mistake. One day, I walked into the CEO's office with a mix of excitement and fear, to ask him, "What if this doesn't work?"

He didn't hesitate and said, "No worries, then we'll find you another role here."

That one sentence changed everything. In that moment, I felt the full weight of trust placed on my shoulders—not as pressure, but as permission. He was saying: Go. Try. Risk. Build. Experiment. And if you stumble, we'll figure it out. That's empowerment.

Empowerment isn't just giving someone the tools. It's giving them belief. It's saying: I see what you can become—and I trust you to get there, even if the path isn't perfect.

The First Real Test

My first sale? A $5,000 web development proposal I pitched with conviction and no pricing model or case studies. I knew we could do it, and they agreed to have us help them build their first association website.

When I returned to the office and told my boss, I was bracing for concern that we weren't charging more. Instead, he simply said, "That's great. Good work!"

Sometimes the greatest strategy is trust.

That wasn't the only leap we took. With each new opportunity, we learned. We modified. We got better.

In one memorable instance, we met with another association's board, still without a formal sales deck. But we showed them something real. It was an online membership directory we had recently developed. After the walkthrough, they looked at us and simply said, "We want that."

That moment didn't just validate our work. It solidified our direction.

Empowerment leads to initiative. Initiative leads to opportunity. And opportunity—when met with trust—creates momentum.

Each sale wasn't simply about revenue. It affirmed something deeper—that trust, experimentation, and genuine empowerment could create growth that was not just scalable, but meaningful.

That early confidence—the muscle strengthened by those initial experiences—became something I relied on throughout my entire career. It wasn't just a skill; it became foundational to my approach to leadership.

A Different Kind of Beginning

And here's the part I didn't tell you in Chapter 1.

That very same project—the one where I was invited to help build the organization's first website—was also the place where I learned what empowerment really looks like in action. It wasn't just about choosing the right visuals or writing clean code. It was about being trusted to figure it out in real time. There was no roadmap. Just a belief that if someone gave me the space and support, I'd rise to the challenge.

Empowerment often starts when someone sees potential in you before you do.

That belief was the spark. What followed was trial, error, growth, and the beginning of my voice as a digital leader.

I was 26 years old, working at the American Association of Neurological Surgeons, when the Assistant Executive Director said: "Can you be on my team to help build our website?"

I remember thinking, What's a website? And why me?

But I was one of the few staff members using a personal computer. That made me the closest thing to "tech-savvy" in the room.

Soon, I was knee-deep in HTML and CSS, learning a language I could barely understand, while helping to build something few associations had ever attempted.

That project wasn't just about tech. It was a crash course in confidence, agility, innovation, creativity, and the power of being trusted before you're ready.

The moment someone believes in you is the moment you start believing in yourself.

The Nine-Year Lab

Empowerment is the oxygen of innovation.

During my nine years at my second association job, I worked under five different CEOs. Some led with trust. Some led with fear.

Here's what I learned:
- Micromanagement kills innovation.
- Control stifles creativity.
- Empowerment activates courage.

The empowering leaders helped their teams take risks, develop ideas, and move forward. Those years became my lab for leadership. Empowerment wasn't just something I experienced. It became the way I chose to lead.

Empowered teams don't wait to be told. They move because they've been trusted.

Empowerment Begins With You

> **You don't need a title to empower others.**
> **You need self-trust.**

With every wave of change, there are always two kinds of people: those who are empowered to create and those who shrink back from what's unfamiliar.

In my 20s, I wasn't handed a manual for confidence. I had to build one. I had to decide I was worth trusting. I had to say yes before I felt ready. That's the shift: Empowerment doesn't start with a policy. It starts with the quiet belief: *I can figure this out.*

You don't need permission. You need intention.

Self-empowerment is the decision to lead from where you stand.

Kevin's Take: The Empowerment Breakdown

We've seen it happen countless times—organizations say they want innovation, but they don't trust their people to make real decisions. They confuse accountability with control. Empowerment doesn't mean letting go of standards. It means investing trust upfront and creating a safety net for growth. And that includes trusting yourself.

—Kevin G. Ordoñez

When Leadership Withholds Power

You can't expect people to act empowered in cultures that punish initiative. Not every organization is designed to empower. Some operate on fear, credit-hoarding, or hierarchy. But even when the system fails you, you can still lead from where you are. I once worked with a client whose manager constantly silenced her.

So, she built her own platform: mentored peers, created a strategy deck, and presented her work in groups. She didn't wait to be invited. She empowered herself. Leadership isn't granted. It's claimed—through action, trust, and courage.

Coaching Leadership to Empower

True empowerment doesn't grow in a vacuum. It begins where leaders have the courage to release control, unlearn old habits, and trust their people. Without that shift, fear takes root—and fear stalls everything. I was working with a client that was launching a major new initiative that required cross-departmental collaboration, real-time decision-making, and trust across all levels of the organization. Instead, what we encountered was fear.

Staff were afraid to speak up. They were afraid to take ownership. They were especially afraid of making a mistake. Why? Because for years, all final decisions—big or small—had been deferred to the senior team. If leaders weren't in the room, progress stalled. Even when staff had great ideas, they held back, fearing criticism, retaliation, or simple dismissal.

At the same time, the senior team was overwhelmed. With too many projects in motion, they couldn't attend all the key meetings, much less provide the real-time feedback required to keep things moving. The system had become a bottleneck—paralyzed not by lack of vision, but by lack of trust.

So, we started with the senior team.

We coached them on what it truly means to empower. That empowerment doesn't mean letting go of oversight, it means letting go of fear. It means trusting that mistakes are part of progress, not signs of failure. We helped them reframe the conversation: What if, instead of fearing mistakes, they normalized learning from them? What if they gave their teams not just responsibilities, but permission?

Then, we worked with the staff.

We held open forums. We talked about fear—naming it, disarming it, and replacing it with clarity. We encouraged team members to step into decisions they were qualified to make. And perhaps most importantly, we ensured they knew they had backup if things went sideways. Leadership wasn't disappearing. They were evolving from gatekeepers to guides.

By the end of the project, everything had shifted.

The initiative was successful, yes—but more importantly, something deeper had changed. Staff were energized. They began stepping into new initiatives with confidence. They asked better questions, took more ownership, and collaborated more freely. And the senior team? They finally had the breathing room to focus on the big-picture strategy they were hired to lead.

Empowerment doesn't mean removing leadership. It means multiplying it.

When people are trusted, they rise. When fear is replaced with faith, teams don't just perform—they innovate.

That's the power of creating a culture where everyone has permission to move the rug.

Rug Reflection:
The Rug We Won't Let Go

This rug keeps us from letting go and stops others from stepping up. To *empower*, we must loosen our grip.

Use the following prompts to journal in the space provided:

- **Where are you holding on so tightly that you're blocking someone else's growth—or your own?**

_____

_____

_____

- **Who needs more ownership than you're currently giving them?**

_____

_____

_____

- **What's one thing you could delegate with trust instead of fear?**

_____

_____

_____

- **Where are you clinging to perfection instead of progress?**

_____

_____

_____

The Practice:
The Empowerment Audit

Empowerment begins with trust—the trust you extend to others. Use this audit to uncover where you may be limiting someone else's growth or holding onto control unnecessarily. Apply what you're learning.

- **List three projects or responsibilities that currently rely on you.**

_____

_____

_____

- **Ask: Is this about their capability—or my control?**

_____

_____

_____

- **Choose one to hand off fully.**

_____

_____

_____

- **Offer guidance, but don't hover. Coach, don't correct.**

_____

_____

_____

The Empowerment Audit:
For Yourself

To empower others, you must notice where you're still leading from control. This audit reveals the places where trust can grow.

Self-trust is the foundation of every bold decision you will make as a leader. Use these questions to examine where you're holding back—and where you're ready to rise.

- **Where am I waiting for permission that I could give myself today?**
  Empowerment begins the moment you stop outsourcing your confidence.

_____

_____

_____

- **What decision have I been delaying because I'm afraid of choosing wrong?**
  Movement creates clarity. Hesitation creates doubt.

_____

_____

_____

- **What have I already proven I can do—but still minimize?**
  List the evidence. You've earned more trust than you're giving yourself.

  _____

  _____

  _____

- **Where am I shrinking in rooms where I should be contributing more boldly?**
  Your voice is part of your value.

  _____

  _____

  _____

- **What opportunity am I almost ready for—and what is one small step toward it?**
  Leaders grow by stepping forward before comfort catches up.

  _____

  _____

  _____

- **What belief is subtly limiting my potential right now?**
  Ask who gave you that belief—and whether you still want to carry it.

  _____

  _____

  _____

- **Where am I holding too tightly out of fear instead of trust?**
  Control feels safe, but it restricts growth—especially your own.

- **How would my leadership shift if I assumed I was capable instead of questioning it?**
  Try leading from that assumption for one day.

- **What risk would I take if I believed I could handle the outcome?**
  Courage is a muscle built through practice.

- **What do I need to hear that no one has said to me yet?**
  Say it to yourself. Say it with conviction. Let your own voice empower you.

Micro-Moves:
Empower Yourself and Others

Empowerment isn't a grand announcement. It's a series of small decisions that signal trust—in yourself and in the people around you. These micro-moves shift a culture from hesitation to momentum.

- **Hand off one decision you've been holding too tightly.**
  Let someone else take the lead, and don't take it back at the first sign of discomfort.

- **Tell someone, "I trust your judgment," and mean it.**
  Clarity creates courage. People rise when they know you believe they can.

- **Ask: "What do you think we should do?"**
  Invite voice before offering direction. Empowerment starts with being heard.

- **Say yes to an opportunity you feel almost ready for.**
  Self-empowerment requires stepping into growth before you feel fully prepared.

- **Replace protection with guidance.**
  Instead of fixing a problem for someone, ask questions that help them solve it themselves.

- **Share the why, then step back.**
  Empowerment thrives when people understand the purpose, not just the task.

- **Remove one approval step that's slowing your team down.**
  Nothing signals trust like eliminating unnecessary checkpoints.

- **Ask yourself: "Am I withholding this responsibility… or is someone ready for it?"**
  Most bottlenecks begin with good intentions and end with stagnation.

- **Celebrate initiative, not just outcomes.**
  People repeat what you recognize. Acknowledging effort builds brave teams.

- **Make one bold move without overthinking.**
  Confidence grows through action, not certainty.

Empowerment expands everything it touches—capacity, confidence, connection. When you practice it daily, you teach your team (and yourself) that growth isn't just allowed. It's expected.

Trust as a Force Multiplier

> **Empowerment isn't something you wait to receive.**
> **It's something you *claim*, *give*, and *become*.**

When that CEO handed me his trust, it wasn't just support—it was strategy. It was a catalyst. So, whether you're leading a team or leading yourself through uncertainty, remember:

Trust is the new currency. Spend it freely.

Because when people feel trusted, they grow. And when they grow, your entire culture shifts.

That's how you *empower* with H.E.A.R.T.

H.E.A.R.T. Summary: EMPOWER

- Let go of control.
- Give people permission to rise.
- Trust yourself to begin.
- Trust others to grow.

Chapter 3:

Ascend – Claiming Your Red-Carpet Moment

"Technology is nothing. What matters is that you have faith in people, that they are basically good and smart and that if you give them tools they will do wonderful things with them."

—Steve Jobs

H.E.A.R.T. Focus:

Ascend – Rise above comfort. Choose growth.

The Rug of Playing Small

Ascension doesn't begin with bold moves. It begins with a whisper: *You can rise.*

And that whisper often comes at the moments when we are trying the hardest to shrink.

Years before grief reshaped my voice, I had already learned this lesson in a quieter way. Early in my career, helping build one of the first websites in the association world taught me something I didn't yet know how to name: I could create something from nothing. We weren't just learning HTML. We were shaping the future before the rest of the sector even realized it was coming. At the time, I thought it was simply a project. Looking back, it was the first proof that I could build what didn't yet exist.

That quiet confidence became the scaffolding for a moment I didn't see coming.

After years of big, demanding work—launching the for-profit business at an association, managing complex projects, navigating multiple CEOs—I reached a point where I wanted something smaller. Simpler. Predictable. I didn't want to lead another major initiative. I wanted to breathe.

So I applied for a project management job.

Not an elevation. A retreat. A job where I could catch my breath and stay safely in the background.

I made it to the third interview. I sat across from the COO, confident he would offer me the role. The relief of stepping into something steady felt so close.

But instead, he looked at me and said, gently but firmly, "You're overqualified. You wouldn't be happy here."

The rug didn't just move—it vanished.

I wasn't trying to rise. I was trying to step back into something smaller. But even the smaller version of me didn't fit anymore.

Walking out of that office, I felt stunned. But underneath the disappointment was a truth I couldn't ignore:

If the smaller path doesn't want you, maybe you weren't meant for small.

So I did the one thing I never expected—I created my own job and started a company. Not because I felt brave. Not because I had a grand vision. But because, for the second time, I realized I could build something from nothing. That belief—first born while building that website—became the foundation of every ascent that followed.

And many years later, it would matter more than I ever imagined.

Because the next time I needed to rise, it wasn't career confusion I was facing. It was heartbreak.

The Voice You Haven't Used Yet

After the death of my husband, followed closely by the losses of my father-in-law and grandmother, and many other tragic events and feeling disappointed by many around me—I found myself in a space I never expected: silenced.

I was still showing up. Still doing the work. But inside, there was nothing. There's a kind of grief that doesn't just take your voice—it takes your belief that you even have one.

I didn't want to hide. But I couldn't figure out how to come forward either.

Then I saw it on my calendar: a keynote I had committed to long before my world came apart.

I didn't cancel. Some quiet, steady part of me—the part that had risen before—knew I needed to show up for the version of myself who said yes to that stage.

That's when I discovered Speaker School.

I logged into the first session with my camera off. I didn't feel ready. I didn't feel visible. I didn't feel like myself.

But as I listened to other women reclaim their confidence, tell their stories, and speak their truth, something in me stirred. They were rising—even through fear, even through uncertainty.

So I turned on my camera.

A small act.

But it was the beginning of my ascent.

Slowly, I began finding a voice I thought I'd lost forever. A voice that could hold grief and growth at the same time. A voice that had risen before—and could rise again.

That's when I finally understood:

Ascension isn't about rising above others.

It's about rising into your fullest self.

> 66 **Kevin's Take: Making Room to Rise**
> Ascension happens when leaders stop trying to do it all themselves. I've seen some of the strongest transformations happen when someone finally lets others speak, step up, or shape a vision. If we want people to rise, we have to clear the space for them to ascend.
> —Kevin G. Ordoñez 99

Rolling Out the Red Carpet

> Growth deserves recognition. Yet most of us skip that step.

We reach a milestone and immediately move toward the next one. We minimize our progress, worried that pausing to celebrate might seem boastful.

But what if we treated every act of courage—no matter how small—like a red-carpet moment?

After my first keynote following Steve's passing, I anticipated feeling relief. What I didn't expect was how powerfully people would celebrate my return to the stage.

It wasn't just applause—it was affirmation. It was their way of saying, *"We see you rising, and we honor your journey."*

That moment taught me something profound:

> When we dare to rise, we illuminate the path for others.
> True leadership isn't about making people follow—
> it's about inspiring them to ascend.

I finally moved that rug and let people see my vulnerability; which, in turn, led to people telling me their stories about how they moved their own rugs to get past their struggles. We will all encounter challenges. My mom always says, "if a group of people in a room all threw their problems in a pile on the floor and had to take one, people would probably just pick their own back up."

Ascending—whether personal or professional—takes courage to move forward. Plus, as leaders, it is important to help others see that they can also ascend and rise from their failures.

I've seen over and over again what happens when people not only identify the rug, but also have the courage to move it. At first, the act is simple—naming what's hidden, acknowledging the pattern, and recognizing what's been tripping them up. But that moment of clarity is powerful. Once the rug is moved, the path forward becomes visible. Growth happens because the obstacles are no longer swept away or ignored.

I think of one leadership team with which I worked that kept tripping over the same issue: Decision making was paralyzed because no one wanted to challenge the board chair. That rug had been sitting there for years, keeping the organization from meeting its true potential. When we finally helped the leaders name the problem, acknowledge it, and create a new structure for healthy debate, the change was immediate. Leaders who had been quiet found their voice, innovation flourished, and the organization began to grow again.

I've also seen the opposite—when people refuse to move the rug. I worked with one group that could clearly see what was holding them back, an outdated business model that drained resources. The group even acknowledged it in meetings. But their fear of conflict and loss kept them from making the necessary change. Those workers kept tripping in the same place, convinced it was safer to stumble than to face what was underneath that rug.

Over time, that avoidance drained their energy, eroded trust, and stalled their growth.

Naming your rug is only the beginning. Transformation comes when you have the courage to move it.

A Different Kind of Ascent

A friend of mine was laid off unexpectedly. She's brilliant, talented, deeply committed—but the loss shook her profoundly. She questioned everything: her worth, her future, even her own voice.

We talked. I reminded her she didn't need to rise all at once; she only needed to take one small step at a time.

And slowly, step by step, she did. She reclaimed her confidence. She rediscovered her voice. Eventually, she found a new job, one more closely aligned with her unique talents and purpose.

Sometimes we ascend not because we feel ready, but because someone else reminds us that we already have everything we need within us.

The Power of Pausing to Celebrate

Several years ago, we helped an organization navigate a major transformation—new leadership, new technology, and a complete reimagining of how they served their members. Morale was fragile. The team was working tirelessly, but no one was pausing long enough to recognize their progress. Everyone felt overwhelmed, behind, and unseen.

During one particularly intense planning session, I asked, "When was the last time you celebrated a win?"

Silence filled the room.

Not one person could recall a recent moment of recognition—no emails of thanks, no shoutouts in meetings, no pauses to honor milestones. They had become so focused on the next challenge that they'd lost sight of how far they'd already come.

So, we introduced a simple practice: *Victory Rounds.*

At the end of every weekly meeting, each team member shared one win, big or small—a successful member call, a resolved issue, an idea that worked.

Initially, it felt awkward. People weren't used to pausing or acknowledging themselves. Many dismissed their accomplishments, unsure if they were "big enough" to celebrate.

But within a month, something shifted.

People began lingering a little longer, looking forward to Victory Rounds. They started taking pride in their progress. Soon, they were highlighting each other's wins, not just their own.

Recognition isn't just celebration—it's fuel.

We watched their culture transform. Initiative grew. Collaboration deepened. The fog of burnout started lifting.

All because we created space to pause, look around, and say clearly: "We see you. And your progress matters."

Sometimes, the most powerful way to help others ascend is simply to acknowledge that they already have.

Ascension is rarely a single moment. It happens in inches—in the choice to speak when silence feels safer, to step forward when retreat seems easier, to rise when life has given you every reason to stay low. Ascending is the practice of believing there is more in you, and then taking one small step that proves it. And when you do, you not only lift yourself—you create a path for others to rise with you. That is the heart of Ascend.

Rug Reflection:
The Rug of Playing Small

Before anyone rises, they must first see the ways they've been holding themselves down. Ascension begins with honesty—the willingness to name the moments where you've stepped back, stayed quiet, or ignored your own potential. These prompts help you see where you may still be standing on a rug that keeps you smaller than the leader you are becoming.

Reflect on the following:

- **Where am I shrinking to make others comfortable—or to avoid being seen?**
  Playing small often feels safer than stepping forward.

  _____

  _____

  _____

- **What opportunity have I talked myself out of because I didn't feel "ready"?**
  Readiness is often a story—not a condition.

  _____

  _____

  _____

- **What part of my voice have I quieted, and why?**
  Your voice is a leadership tool. Silence carries a cost.

  _____

  _____

  _____

- **Where am I waiting for permission instead of trusting what I already know?**
  Ascension begins the moment you stop deferring your own wisdom.

  _____

  _____

  _____

- **What belief about myself is keeping me anchored to an old identity?**
  Growth requires a new internal narrative.

  _____

  _____

  _____

- **What would rising look like for me right now—not someday, not later, but now?**
  Clarity opens the path.

  _____

  _____

  _____

Rug Reflection:
For Your Team

The rugs that hold teams back are often different from the ones we confront personally. They show up as unspoken norms, outdated hierarchies, unclear expectations, or a culture that rewards silence more than contribution. Use these reflections to see where your team may be tripping.

- **Where does our team hesitate to speak up, contribute, or challenge the status quo?**
  And what does that hesitation reveal about safety, trust, or culture?

_____

_____

_____

- **Who is playing small because we haven't created space for them to rise?**
  Talent shrinks when leaders dominate the room.

_____

_____

_____

- **What outdated expectations or norms make it harder for people to step into new roles or ideas?**
  Teams ascend when old structures loosen.

  _____

  _____

  _____

- **What accomplishments are we skipping past instead of celebrating?**
  Recognition is oxygen for collective ascension.

  _____

  _____

  _____

- **Where are decisions bottlenecked at the top?**
  A team cannot rise if authority never moves down.

  _____

  _____

  _____

- **What would happen if we rolled out the red carpet for someone else's growth this week?**
  Ascension multiplies when it's shared.

  _____

  _____

  _____

The Practice:
Your Growth Gap

Apply what you're learning.

- **Write where you are today—in your voice, your confidence, your leadership.**

_____

_____

_____

Now, imagine where you want to be in six months.

- **What's one habit, belief, or fear that stands in your way?**

_____

_____

_____

- **What's one micro-action you can take this week?**

_____

_____

_____

Micro-Moves:
Ascend With Confidence and Courage

Ascension is not about hierarchy. It's about stepping into your full voice and helping others rise into theirs. Small acts of courage compound into transformation.

- **Turn your camera on when you instinctively want to hide.**
  Visibility is a choice you make long before the world sees your value.

- **Speak once in every meeting—even if it's brief.**
  Your voice gets stronger each time you use it.

- **Encourage someone else to take the spotlight.**
  Say, "You should present this. It's your win." Elevation multiplies when shared.

- **Share one idea before you've polished it.**
  Perfection isn't where growth begins. Openness is.

- **Say the thing you've been rehearsing in your head.**
  Courage often sounds like one honest sentence.

- **Acknowledge your progress out loud.**
  Not bragging—truth-telling. "I've grown here, and I'm proud of it."

- **Ask for the opportunity instead of waiting to be noticed.**
  Closed mouths don't get invitations. Ascension requires self-advocacy.

- **Celebrate someone else's ascent publicly.**
  Your voice can become the platform someone else stands on.

- **Do something that scares you for five minutes.**
  File the application. Hit publish. Introduce yourself. Confidence grows through exposure.

- **Replace self-doubt with one grounding affirmation.**
  Not empty positivity—a truth: "I've done hard things before. I can do this too."

Rising happens in moments most people overlook. When you choose courage in small ways, you build the muscle that carries you through the big ones—and you signal to others that they're allowed to rise too.

The Courage to Climb

Disruption doesn't stop. Neither does doubt. But neither does your ability to *choose growth*.

"It's not what shows up. It's how YOU show up."
—Tim Shurr, MA, Author, *One Belief Away*

Every day brings a new moment to decide who you're becoming. Sometimes that choice is loud—standing on a stage, speaking truth, taking a risk. Other times, it's quiet—getting out of bed when it's easier to hide, turning your camera on, reaching out when you'd rather retreat.

You don't need to be fearless to rise. You just need to be willing.

Ascension isn't a grand gesture. It's a practice. A daily decision to meet uncertainty with presence, to meet challenge with openness, to meet your life as it is and still move forward, one step at a time.

That's how you ascend with H.E.A.R.T.—not once, but continually. Because the real climb isn't upward; it's inward. Every step you take toward your highest self makes it easier for others to rise too.

H.E.A.R.T. Summary: ASCEND

- Step into growth.
- Reclaim your voice.
- Show up—even if your voice shakes.
- Celebrate your rise and make space for others to rise too.

Chapter 4:

Reimagine – The Rug of Routine

"Forget past mistakes. Forget failures. Forget everything
except what you're going to do now—and do it."
—WILLIAM DURANT, co-founder, General Motors

H.E.A.R.T. Focus:
Reimagine – Challenge the familiar. See new possibilities.

Transformation doesn't always require reinvention. Sometimes, it begins
with one disruptive question:

> **You don't need all the answers to begin.**
> **You just need the courage to ask a better question.**

What if there's a better way?

This question is the spark that ignites reimagination. It's the moment we
stop stepping over outdated systems, habits, and assumptions like rugs
we've learned to ignore—and start wondering why they're there at all.

Routine thinking is just like that rug. It's the comfort of the
known—the repetition of the default. It's the illusion that doing what
we've always done is the safest bet.

But comfort is deceptive. Routine gives us the illusion of control. It promises predictability. It tells us that if we follow the rules, we'll get the same results. However, the world is no longer the same as it used to be—the world has changed. Therefore, the longer we cling to the way things were, the more we block what could be.

What If We Don't Shut It Down?

Years ago, we worked with a non-profit company planning to shut down its for-profit creative services division. On paper, it made sense: declining revenue, outdated models, limited staff.

However, when we met the team, we saw more than a sunsetting service line. We saw possibility. These weren't just designers. They were communicators, collaborators, and storytellers. So, we asked:

—What if we didn't shut it down?

—What if we reimagined its purpose?

The CEO took the risk. That team evolved into a digital transformation engine. Their reimagined role became central to the organization's future.

Reimagination is not about discarding what was—it's about discovering what still can be.

Innovation Isn't Always Invention

We often believe innovation requires building from scratch. However, some of the most profound changes come from reworking what already exists.

One organization planned to dismantle its learning platform due to poor engagement. However, after conducting customer interviews, we discovered that the problem wasn't the content—it was the lack of relevance. We didn't rebuild. We repackaged. Personalized. Layered in AI for smarter navigation. Engagement soared.

Innovation can start by asking: What already works—and how can we make it work better?

During the pandemic, we all became *reimaginers*—whether we wanted to or not. We reimagined how we parented, worked, learned, and even grieved. The organizations that adapted quickly didn't wait for stability. They embraced imagination as a survival skill.

Reimagining Under Pressure

Midway through a major system implementation for a client, the project was sinking. The consulting firm that originally led the effort had missed deadline after deadline. What was supposed to be a transformational launch had dragged on for over a year, and the finish line felt further away than ever.

Staff described the project as "a treadmill we can't get off." In one particularly raw conversation, a department head told me, "We don't even believe it'll ever launch anymore."

It wasn't just timelines that had been lost—it was trust.

That's when we were called in.

We were tasked with assessing the situation and, if possible, getting the ship back on course. The pressure was high. Leadership was considering pulling the plug entirely. Nevertheless, as we dug in, it became clear: the problem wasn't the technology—it was the process.

That's where we made a bold recommendation.

Reassign your top internal talent—yes, even if it means pausing other priorities. Build a cross-functional sprint team. Give them space to focus solely on the system launch. Let us lead with a simplified and agile approach.

There was hesitation. This wasn't how they were used to operating. They had never done something like this before, but leadership said yes. That single decision created a turning point. Not only was the system launched on time—without major disruption to members—but something more important happened: inside the organization, belief was restored.

It wasn't just a technology win. It was a cultural reset. A moment when reimagination meant refusing to accept slow failure—and choosing decisive momentum instead.

You can honor the past and still rewrite the future.

Sometimes, the system doesn't need to be replaced, it needs rethinking.

Kevin's Take: The Danger of Standing Still

One of the most revealing engagements I've had was with a legacy nonprofit that had weathered disruption for decades. But when it came time to rethink their governance and membership model, they refused. They'd been doing it 'their way' for 30 years—and that comfort eventually became their constraint. They lost members. They lost relevance.

And eventually, they came back—not because they wanted to innovate, but because they couldn't afford not to. Reimagination is a choice—until it becomes a requirement.

—Kevin G. Ordoñez

Reimagining After Loss

After Steve passed away, I had to reimagine everything: parenting, leadership, my sense of self.

Not because I wanted to. Because life gave me no other choice.

You can grieve what was and still design what's next.

At first, it felt impossible, like I was trying to sketch a new map while grieving the one that had guided me for years. Every role I had—wife, mother, entrepreneur, leader—suddenly felt unfamiliar. I knew who I had been, but I wasn't sure who I was becoming.

There were mornings I couldn't see beyond the next hour. But slowly, I started to ask new questions. Not "How do I get back to where I was?" but "What could this look like now?" and "What would healing on my own terms require?"

That shift in mindset didn't erase the grief, but it gave me something to build on. I reimagined how I worked, giving myself space and grace. I reimagined how I showed up for my daughters, choosing presence over perfection. I reimagined how I led, bringing more empathy and honesty into the room.

Every reimagined life begins with one brave moment of letting go.

Reimagination doesn't deny loss or what worked well in the past. It honors what was—while daring to believe that what's next can still be meaningful. Even beautiful.

What if healing isn't returning to normal? What if it's discovering a new kind of beauty?

Just as I had to reimagine my identity beyond loss, organizations must reimagine their purpose beyond tradition. The playbook won't always serve us. Sometimes, we have to write a new one.

Reimagining isn't about erasing your story. It's about expanding it.

In a time of disruption, reimagination is both strategy and survival. It's how we lead forward, not with certainty, but with vision.

When everything changes, reimagining is an act of hope. You don't have to know exactly what comes next. You only need to be willing to believe there's always another way.

Imagination as a Leadership Practice

Imagination isn't a luxury reserved for creative moments—it's a discipline leaders must cultivate every day. When you question routines, explore possibilities, and challenge assumptions, you strengthen the muscle that keeps your organization adaptable and alive. In a world that rewards efficiency, imagination is often the first thing leaders abandon and the last thing they realize they need. Reimagination becomes a leadership practice when you stay curious, stay courageous, and stay willing to see beyond what already exists.

Rug Reflection:
The Rug of Routine Thinking

Reimagination isn't about tearing everything down. It's about refusing to accept routine as truth. Every organization—and every leader—carries assumptions that once served a purpose but have quietly become barriers to what's next. These reflections help you surface those hidden constraints, question the familiar, and open the door to new possibilities.

- **What process or assumption have I accepted without question?**
  Routine becomes rug-like when it stops being examined.

_____

_____

_____

- **Where have I stopped asking, "Why are we doing it this way?"**
  Silence often protects outdated thinking.

_____

_____

_____

- **What system, belief, or habit might be limiting our growth?**
  Not all constraints are external.

_____

_____

_____

- **What part of our strategy or culture are we defending simply because it's familiar?**
  Comfort often masquerades as wisdom.

  _____

  _____

  _____

- **What question am I avoiding because I already know the answer might require change?**
  Reimagination begins at the edge of our discomfort.

  _____

  _____

  _____

- **What assumptions are baked into our team or organization that no one has challenged in years?**
  If everything is assumed, nothing is reimagined.

  _____

  _____

  _____

- **Where have we mistaken tradition for strategy?**
  Legacy isn't automatically leadership.

  _____

  _____

  _____

- **What possibility have I dismissed too quickly?**
  Innovation often starts with ideas that feel "too big."

- **What unmet need are our members, customers, or stakeholders quietly signaling?**
  Reimagination starts by noticing what is no longer working.

- **What would we build if we were starting from scratch today?**
  This question unlocks authentic creativity.

- **Where are we stepping over an organizational rug because addressing it would require conflict or courage?**
  Avoidance preserves the problem.

- **What do I sense is ready to evolve—even if no one has said it out loud yet?**
  Leaders often feel the shift before they can articulate it.

  _____

  _____

  _____

- **What idea or opportunity feels energizing—and why haven't we explored it?**
  Energy is a compass pointing toward reimagination.

  _____

  _____

  _____

- **What are we protecting that may no longer deserve protection?**
  Sometimes the sacred cow is actually slowing the herd.

  _____

  _____

  _____

The Practice:
10-Star Thinking

Reimagination doesn't require sweeping disruption. It begins with curiosity—the willingness to explore beyond the obvious and challenge what you've grown accustomed to. One of the simplest ways to unlock expansive thinking is to temporarily remove constraints and imagine a version of your work that exceeds expectations by a wide margin.

Choose a program, process, meeting, customer experience, event, or service your team delivers today. Then ask:

- **What would a five-star version look like?**

_____

_____

_____

- **A seven-star version?**

_____

_____

_____

- **A 10-star version?**

_____

_____

_____

Stretch the vision. Then reverse-engineer one bold improvement you can act on.

Micro-Moves: Reimagine What's Possible

Reimagination doesn't begin with a blank slate. It begins with one disrupted assumption at a time. These micro-moves create the space for fresh thinking and new solutions.

- **Ask one disruptive question in your next meeting.**
  "What if we didn't do it this way?"

- **Challenge one assumption you've been carrying.**
  Ask: "Who told me this had to be true?"

- **Flip a routine task on its head.**
  Try a different order, format, or approach.

- **Invite someone with a different perspective into the conversation.**
  Fresh eyes often surface hidden possibilities.

- **Replace "We can't" with "What would it take?"**
  Possibility unlocks innovation.

- **Review one process and ask: "If we built this today, would we build it this way?"**
  Legacy habits survive only when unexamined.

- **Give yourself permission to explore before committing.**
  Sketch. Brainstorm. Try on ideas.

- **Read or listen to something outside your field.**
  Innovation is often imported.

- **Notice where your energy spikes.**
  Interest is a compass for creativity.

- **Take one small risk that nudges you out of routine.**
  Message the collaborator. Pitch the idea. Test the concept.

Reimagination doesn't demand reinvention. It requires curiosity—and the courage to take the smallest possible step beyond what is familiar.

H.E.A.R.T. Summary: REIMAGINE

- Challenge defaults.
- Ask better questions.
- Elevate curiosity into courage.
- Lead through bold possibility.

Chapter 5:

Transform – The Rug We Outgrew

"You are one belief away from your breakthrough."
— Tim Shurr, MA, Author, *One Belief Away*

H.E.A.R.T. Focus:
Transform – Let go of the old. Become who you are meant to be.

Transformation isn't about bouncing back. It's about breaking through.

When Steve died, everything I knew about myself, and my world collapsed overnight. One day, I was delivering keynotes, leading strategy sessions, and managing both my company and family life. The next, I was staring at an empty chair at our dinner table, the silence echoing loudly. Every familiar routine, every comforting plan, dissolved. That year, it seemed that every month something terrible happened.

Outwardly, I continued showing up for work, but inwardly, I was numb—unanchored. Like a story without a narrator, I felt disconnected from my own life.

I knew I needed help but wasn't sure where to find it.

One afternoon, scrolling through Facebook, I saw a post from a high school friend—Tim Shurr, a professional coach and therapist. Something nudged me to reach out. Tim introduced me to his "One Belief Away" method, and our work together changed everything.

Tim helped me see how many of my core beliefs were rooted deeply in survival. I'd spent years building an identity around being strong, capable, dependable. But beneath that strength was a quiet fear whispering, *"If you let go, everything will collapse."*

That belief had served me—until it didn't.

Tim helped me loosen the grip of that fear. I shifted from asking, *"What if I fail?"* to *"What if this works?"* I learned to be strong not only for others but, finally, for myself.

This shift didn't erase grief. Instead, it created the space for genuine growth.

From Surviving to Sherry 2.0

That transformation marked the beginning of what I now call *Sherry 2.0.*

I wasn't shinier. I wasn't perfect. I was simply whole.

I wasn't a reinvention. I was a return—to my voice, my purpose, and my strength. But this time, it was more grounded. More present. More aligned with who I had always been—and who I was becoming.

I wasn't just guiding organizations through transformation. I was embodying it. Leading from within.

As Sherry 2.0, I knew that telling my story wasn't a weakness, it was an offering. A way to reach others still buried under their own rugs of grief, burnout, fear, rejection, or silence.

I began speaking more openly about what I had experienced—not just the professional milestones, but also the personal battles that had tested my strength. And something remarkable happened: People leaned in. They saw themselves reflected in my journey, realizing they weren't alone or stuck.

That's how coaching found me.

I wasn't looking for another role. But after everything I'd faced, helping others navigate their own transformations became a passion and a calling. In every workshop, keynote, and coaching session, I wasn't showing up as someone who had all the answers. I was showing up as someone who had walked through fire and chose to rise.

Because true transformation isn't about becoming someone else.

It's about fully becoming who you already are.

What Transformation Really Means

Real transformation requires shedding old beliefs and rewiring your identity. It asks you to choose purpose and possibility over comfort and familiarity.

We often see transformation as strategic—a shift in technology, goals, or KPIs But true transformation isn't tidy. It's deeply personal. It's emotional. It begins from within.

Transformation begins when we have the courage to see what's truly beneath the surface—to notice what we're tripping over. We all carry limiting beliefs that silently shape our decisions.

Not long after my husband passed away, I was invited to give a keynote. Every part of me wanted to say no. The grief was still raw, and the voice in my head kept repeating, "What if I can't hold it together? What if I fail in front of everyone?"

For weeks, I wrestled with that fear. Then I asked myself a different question: "What if this is the opportunity to step back into my voice? What if this is the moment that helps me rise again?"

Walking onto that stage was terrifying, but it became a turning point. By leaning into the possibility of growth instead of collapse, I found strength I didn't know I had.

That experience taught me something crucial: the path forward isn't about ignoring our doubts—it's about transforming them.

When you catch yourself wondering, "What if I fall?" reframe it as, "What if this is the opportunity that changes everything?"

When that inner voice insists, "I'm not ready for this," challenge it with, "What's one step I can take right now to move forward?"

That choice didn't erase the pain, but it reminded me that transformation begins the moment we decide to see fear not as a barrier, but as a doorway to what's next.

For more than 30 years, I've guided organizations through digital and organizational change, helping them modernize legacy systems, shift outdated mindsets, and future-proof their strategies. But the most profound transformations I've witnessed never begin with technology. They begin with people, beliefs, and culture.

And I learned this firsthand when I had to transform my own life.

Kevin's Take: Identity Isn't Fixed—It Evolves
The greatest leadership trap is believing your title defines your contribution. The most impactful leaders evolve their identity as their purpose grows. They don't cling to past achievements; instead, they ask, 'Who does this season require me to become?' Real transformation happens when we accept that our identity isn't static—it's a living expression of our values.

—Kevin G. Ordoñez

A Professional Parallel:
The Organization That Rewrote Itself

We once worked with an organization deeply stuck in its own story. Engagement was low. Energy was depleted. They had tried everything— except addressing the core issue: identity.

They saw themselves as slow, traditional, and risk averse. Legacy beliefs echoed:

- "We've never done that."
- "Our members won't embrace change."
- "That's just not who we are."

During a strategy session, we asked a simple but powerful question:

"If you were just starting this organization today, what would it look like?"

That question cracked open something transformative. They restructured, piloted bold initiatives, rebuilt technology, and, most importantly, reimagined their identity.

Their transformation wasn't flashy. It was fundamental.

Just like mine.

Designing the Next Chapter

Transformation isn't about fixing yourself. It's about consciously designing a life that honors who you've become.

After losing Steve, I had to reimagine everything—parenting, running a business, how I showed up each day. Eventually, I asked myself:

"What now? What is this next season meant for?"

Organizations, too, must reimagine who they are beyond titles, structures, and traditions. Culture is the invisible script we live by— until we choose to rewrite it.

Transformation isn't about discarding everything that came before. It's about evolving intentionally, consciously, and courageously.

Transformation isn't returning. *It's becoming.*

Leading in the Now

We can't lead from the past or control the future. We can only lead from here, in this present moment.

Regret lives in the past. Anxiety lives in the future. Leadership lives in the now.

Presence is foundational to transformation. Mindfulness, reflection, taking deep breaths—these are leadership tools as powerful as any strategy or technology.

As Kevin often says, "Too many leaders live in the rearview or on a distant map. But real transformation happens now."

When we fully embrace the present—in our pain, our growth, our leadership—we gain something extraordinary: the clarity to respond thoughtfully, not habitually. The courage to evolve intentionally, rather than merely react.

True leadership lives here. In this very moment.

And the greatest leaders understand clearly: THIS moment is where true transformation begins.

The Ripple Effect of H.E.A.R.T.

You've named your rugs.

You've uncovered what's been hiding beneath them.

You've begun to move what once held you back.

That work alone is transformational.

But the true power of H.E.A.R.T. doesn't end with you.

It expands—quietly, steadily, and unmistakably—into the lives of the people around you.

That is the ripple effect.

When you humanize yourself, it becomes easier to humanize others.

When you empower yourself, you naturally empower your team.

When you ascend, you show others they can rise too.

When you reimagine what's possible, your organization begins to imagine with you.

And when you transform, you create space for others to do the same.

The ripple begins inside—but it never stays there.

Through this work, we've watched people turn negative thoughts into positive beliefs, break down what's been holding them back, and step into a stronger, clearer version of themselves. And as each person rises, something remarkable happens: their courage gives permission for others to rise too.

This is where leadership shifts from personal development to cultural impact.

This is where H.E.A.R.T. becomes more than a framework—it becomes a way of leading forward.

The greatest leaders aren't remembered for how perfectly they stood.

They're remembered for how many people they helped rise.

You've moved your rug.

Now it's time to help others move theirs.

Let's move forward—together.

Rug Reflection:
The Rug of Identity

We often cling to an old identity long after it has stopped serving us. Transformation asks us to examine the beliefs beneath our behavior— the quiet stories we tell ourselves about who we need to be to belong, succeed, or survive. These reflections help you name what you've outgrown and see what's ready to emerge.

- **Where am I holding onto an identity that no longer fits the leader I am becoming?**
  Growth requires releasing roles that once defined you.

_____

_____

_____

- **What belief is keeping me anchored to a past version of myself?**
  Most rugs of identity are woven from outdated stories.

_____

_____

_____

- **Where am I over-delivering to prove my worth—
  and to whom?**
  Effort rooted in fear is not the same as leadership rooted in truth.

- **What part of me is asking for permission to evolve?**
  Every transformation begins with a quiet internal request.

- **What expectation, role, or persona am I afraid to let go of?**
  Fear is often a sign of exactly where transformation wants to take place.

- **What would it feel like to lead from who I am now—not
  who I've been?**
  Your next chapter requires your present self, not your past one.

- **What belief would I release today if I trusted myself more fully?**
  Transformation begins with one belief changing shape.

_____

_____

_____

Rug Reflection:
Transforming Your Team's Identity

Just as individuals cling to outdated beliefs about who they need to be, teams and organizations hold on to identities that once helped them succeed but now limit their growth. Cultural transformation begins when leaders are willing to examine not only their own beliefs, but the collective ones their teams carry. These questions help you see where your organization may be ready to evolve.

- **What identity has our team outgrown—but continues to perform out of habit?**
  Old stories create new limitations.

  _____

  _____

  _____

- **What belief about "how we operate" is no longer true but still shapes our decisions?**
  Cultures often obey rules no one remembers writing.

  _____

  _____

  _____

- **Where are we over-delivering to maintain an image that no longer serves us?**
  Teams cling to proving themselves long after they've earned trust.

  _____

  _____

  _____

- **What fear keeps us anchored to models, structures, or practices we've outlived?**
  Most cultural rugs stay in place because they're familiar, not because they're useful.

  _____

  _____

  _____

- **What capability do we have now that contradicts the identity we're still holding onto?**
  Transformation begins where identity catches up to capacity.

  _____

  _____

  _____

- **What belief would our team release if it trusted its own potential more deeply?**
  Organizational self-doubt is real—and reversible.

  _____

  _____

  _____

- **Who do we need to become to lead our members, customers, or community into the future?**
  Transformation is directional—identity must point toward what's next.

  _____

  _____

  _____

The Practice:
The Old Me / New Me Manifesto

Transformation becomes real the moment you name the identity you're releasing and the one you're choosing next. This isn't about becoming someone different—it's about stepping into who you were always capable of being.

Apply what you're learning.

Write your identity shift. Complete the following:

- **"The old me believed ..."**

_____

_____

_____

- **"The new me chooses ..."**

_____

_____

_____

- **Write three to five of these. Say them out loud. Post them somewhere you'll see them daily.**

_____

_____

_____

The Practice:
Team Identity Shift

Every team operates from an internal story—a shared identity that shapes decisions, communication, risk tolerance, and performance. Sometimes that identity is empowering. Sometimes it's inherited, outdated, or unconsciously limiting. Transforming a team begins with bringing that story into the light.

Use this practice to help your team uncover—and update—the identity that drives how they lead, work, and show up together.

Step 1:
Name the Old Story

Ask your team:

"If we had to describe who we've been as a team, in one sentence, what would it be?"

Listen for words like:

- cautious
- overextended
- traditional
- scrappy
- reactive
- siloed
- service-oriented
- compliant
- over-reliant on leadership

These reveal the *current* identity—not the desired one.

Step 2:
Identify the Impact

Discuss:

"How has this identity helped us? And how has it held us back?"

Affirm the past.
Acknowledge the limits.
No shame—just truth.

Step 3:
Define the New Version

Ask the transformative question:
"Who do we need to become to lead the future effectively?"
This anchors the identity shift in purpose, not aspiration.

Step 4:
Choose One Behavioral Shift

Transformation doesn't happen all at once.
It begins with one simple, concrete change.
Ask:
"What is one behavior we can adopt this month that reflects the team we want to become?"
Examples:

- Speaking up earlier
- Sharing wins
- Making faster decisions
- Asking better questions
- Taking turns leading meetings
- Challenging assumptions respectfully

Step 5:
Make It Visible

Close with:
"What does this new identity look like in action?"
Turn the abstract identity shift into observable behavior.
Transformation sticks when the story becomes something the team can see itself living into.

Micro-Moves:
Transform From the Inside Out

Transformation doesn't begin with reinvention. It begins with honesty—the courage to see what no longer fits and the willingness to choose differently. These micro-moves help you loosen the grip of old beliefs and take small steps toward the leader you're becoming.

- **Let go of one outdated belief today.**
  Say it out loud: "This no longer serves me." Naming it breaks its grip.

- **Replace one limiting thought with a truer one.**
  Shift from "I have to hold everything together" to "I can ask for support."

- **Choose one behavior that belongs to your next chapter—and practice it once.**
  Future identity grows through present action.

- **Share a moment of growth with someone you trust.**
  Transformation becomes real when witnessed.

- **Admit when something is no longer working.**
  Endings are catalysts, not failures.

- **Ask for help where you normally power through alone.**
  Receiving support is a transformational act.

- **Release one task, role, or expectation you've outgrown.**
  Clearing space is often the first step in becoming someone new.

- **Try a new response to an old trigger.**
  Transformation shows up in the gap between stimulus and choice.

- **Reflect on a time you overcame something difficult.**
  Your evidence of resilience becomes fuel for what's next.

- **Speak one truth you've been avoiding.**
  Authenticity cracks open the doorway to real transformation.

Transformation rarely arrives in sweeping moments. It happens in subtle shifts—the small decisions that gradually rewrite your identity, your leadership, and your life. When you change your beliefs by inches, your world eventually changes by miles.

Micro-Moves:
Evolve Together

Evolution happens when individual growth becomes collective momentum. These micro-moves help you nurture a culture where people learn, adapt, and rise—not because they're told to, but because they feel supported in becoming their best selves.

- **Ask one person, "What rug are you tripping over that I can help move?"**
  Support becomes culture when it's proactive, not reactive.

- **Share something you've recently learned—and how it changed your perspective.**
  When leaders learn out loud, teams feel safer to grow.

- **Invite a team member to improve a process you've always owned.**
  Evolution accelerates when power is shared.

- **Admit one mistake publicly.**
  Imperfection normalizes experimentation far better than any policy.

- **Establish one new ritual that reinforces H.E.A.R.T.**
  A weekly win-share, a pause for gratitude, a 10-minute check-in—habits become culture.

- **Ask for feedback on your leadership.**
  Your willingness to evolve makes evolution safe for everyone else.

- **Mentor someone informally.**
  A five-minute conversation can reroute a career.

- **Give someone credit publicly for their idea or initiative.**
  Recognition seeds confidence. Confidence fuels evolution.

- **Revisit one long-standing practice and ask the team, "Does this still serve us?"**
  Evolution thrives when nothing is off-limits for improvement.

- **Model calm during uncertainty.**
  Your presence becomes the anchor others evolve around.

Organizations evolve when people evolve—and people evolve when the environment signals that growth is not just allowed, but expected and supported. These micro-moves remind your team that leadership is a shared responsibility and a shared opportunity.

Becoming Who You Were Meant to Be

Transformation isn't a plan. It's a process. A surrender of certainty. A decision to stop living by an outdated script.

Every transformation asks for a letting go before it gives back.

Sherry 2.0 didn't emerge because I had a new plan. She emerged because I let go of the old one.

Whether it's an individual stepping into a new version of themselves or an organization navigating the AI era, transformation requires a mindset shift—not just new tools, but new truths. Not just different work, but a different way of being.

You don't need to reinvent yourself. You just need to recognize the evolution already within you.

Growth isn't a leap; it's the quiet realization that you already crossed the line.

That's how you transform—with H.E.A.R.T.

H.E.A.R.T. Summary: TRANSFORM

- Redefine your identity.
- Loosen outdated beliefs.
- Act with presence.
- Build what aligns with who you are now.

Chapter 6:

Evolve – Multiplying H.E.A.R.T. Through Others

"Your legacy as a leader isn't built by what you achieve alone. It's built by who you lift, empower, and inspire to lead after you."

—SHERRY WHITAKER BUDZIAK

Transformation begins within, but it doesn't end there. The most powerful growth happens when your inner evolution becomes an outer force for change.

From Inner Work to Outer Impact

I used to think leadership meant being the smartest person in the room. I stayed late. Knew the answers. Prided myself on never dropping the ball. Then one day, a team member came to me, not for answers, but for belief.

That moment changed me. I realized leadership isn't about what you carry—it's about what you help others rise to carry.

By now, you've moved your rug. You've confronted old beliefs. You've learned to trust yourself. You've transformed from the inside out.

Now it's time for the next evolution: Helping others do the same.

Culture Doesn't Happen by Accident

One of the biggest myths in leadership is that culture "just happens." But culture isn't an accident. It's an accumulation of choices, conversations, and character.

You don't lead culture with perks. You lead it with presence.

You model H.E.A.R.T.:

- **Humanize** your leadership interactions with empathy and vulnerability.
- **Empower** your teams by transferring trust and decision-making.
- **Ascend** others by encouraging growth and risk.
- **Reimagine** systems, not just preserve legacy processes.
- **Transform** by sharing your own evolution and inviting others into theirs.

H.E.A.R.T. isn't policy. It's a daily practice.

And you don't need a title to lead with H.E.A.R.T. Some of the most powerful culture-shapers are individual contributors who ask hard questions, lift others up, and model courage behind the scenes.

The Rug of Bottleneck Leadership

We say we want innovation, but we review every decision. We say we want empowered teams, yet we hoard the authority. We claim to trust our people, yet we micromanage the outcomes. Sometimes the rug we need to move is ourselves.

The Culture Cascade

As Kevin and I often say, "Culture flows downhill—but character climbs uphill."

If you humanize others, they will, too. If you empower them, they will take ownership. If you reimagine, others will innovate. If you transform, others will follow.

You can't ask for boldness while rewarding obedience. You can't demand resilience while punishing mistakes. You must *be* the culture you want to see.

That's what true leadership is. Leaders create space for others to discover what's possible.

Ask yourself: Am I making it easier or harder for others to lead?

Kevin's Take: H.E.A.R.T. as a Culture Strategy
When organizations commit to H.E.A.R.T., they stop treating culture like a side project and start treating it like a strategic superpower. Culture is not soft—it's structural. It determines whether innovation sticks, whether leaders thrive, and whether people rise or retreat.

—Kevin G. Ordoñez

A Real-World Transformation Story

We worked with organizations that had all the right words on paper: empowerment, innovation, inclusion, but reality didn't match. Teams were afraid to speak. Risk-taking was quietly punished. Trust was thin.

It wasn't malicious. It was just unexamined.

Through workshops and coaching, we uncovered their cultural "rugs": outdated hierarchies, fear of failure, lack of psychological safety.

The shift didn't come from new policies. It came from new behavior:

- Leaders praised effort, not just outcomes.
- They shared their own mistakes.
- They asked for feedback—and meant it.

Within a year, employee engagement rose 30 percent. Retention improved. Trust flourished.

Culture wasn't declared. It was demonstrated.

Rug Reflection:
The Rug of Unquestioned Inheritance

We don't always choose the rugs we stand on. Many are inherited—passed down through policies, traditions, unspoken expectations, and cultural habits that were created long before we arrived. Evolving as a leader means examining those inherited patterns and deciding which ones deserve to continue and which ones quietly keep us from growing.

Use the following prompts to journal in the space provided:

- **What habits or assumptions have I inherited without examining?**
  Inherited beliefs often become invisible barriers.

  _____

  _____

  _____

- **Where am I upholding a standard simply because "it's always been that way"?**
  Tradition becomes a rug the moment it stops serving people.

  _____

  _____

  _____

- **What systems feel comfortable to me, but create barriers for others?**
  Comfort is not the same as effectiveness.

- **What part of my team or organizational culture needs unwinding before it can be rebuilt?**
  You cannot evolve around a pattern that you refuse to name.

- **Where do I see myself or my team drifting back into old behaviors—and why?**
  Regression is often a sign that a deeper belief still needs attention.

- **Which inherited expectations no longer align with who we are becoming?**
  Evolution requires letting go as much as building up.

  _____

  _____

  _____

- **What new identity or behavior needs reinforcement so it becomes a norm, not a moment?**
  Change becomes culture through repetition.

  _____

  _____

  _____

The Practice:
H.E.A.R.T.-Based Culture Audit

Evolving a team or organization requires more than personal insight. It requires looking honestly at the culture you are shaping—intentionally or not. Use this audit to assess how well your environment reflects the principles of H.E.A.R.T. and where your leadership can reinforce the path forward.

Complete this audit with honesty and courage.

Culture does not change by accident—it changes by attention, intention, and repetition.

- **H – Humanize**
  How does our culture acknowledge people's humanity—not just their output?
  Where do empathy, presence, and genuine connection need more space?

_____

_____

_____

_____

_____

- **E – Empower**
  Where are decisions still overly centralized—and what could we release?
  Cultures evolve when trust grows.

  _____

  _____

  _____

  _____

  _____

- **A – Ascend**
  How are we creating clear, visible opportunities for people to grow?
  Who is rising—and who is being unintentionally held down?

  _____

  _____

  _____

  _____

  _____

- **R – Reimagine**
What legacy norms, expectations, or processes no longer serve who we are becoming?
What needs to be retired so something better can take its place?

_____

_____

_____

_____

- **T – Transform**
How do we model learning, adaptation, and evolution—especially when it's uncomfortable?
Teams follow leaders who are visibly growing themselves.

_____

_____

_____

_____

Micro-Moves:
Evolve Together

Evolution isn't a dramatic leap. It's the steady, disciplined practice of reinforcing what matters and refusing to slip back into what once felt familiar. These micro-moves help you strengthen the culture you're building—one intentional action at a time.

- **Reaffirm one H.E.A.R.T. principle in a real conversation.**
  Name it out loud. Culture grows from what leaders reinforce consistently.

- **Catch one "old habit" as it shows up—and choose differently.**
  Awareness is the first safeguard against regression.

- **Invite someone into a decision you would normally make alone.**
  Shared ownership is the engine of cultural evolution.

- **Celebrate one small example of cultural growth this week.**
  What gets recognized gets repeated.

- **Revisit a norm, expectation, or process and ask, "Does this still serve who we're becoming?"**
  Evolution accelerates when leaders stay curious.

- **Create one opening for someone else to lead.**
  A rotating facilitator, a delegated responsibility, a spotlight moment.

- **Model transparency once today.**
  Share what you're learning, unlearning, or reconsidering. Evolution spreads through honesty.

- **Replace certainty with inquiry at least once.**
  Instead of providing the answer, ask a question that sparks thinking.

- **Protect time for reflection—individually and as a team.**
  Cultures evolve when people have space to see their progress.

- **Identify one behavior that represents the future culture— and practice it intentionally.**
  Small actions shape identity. Repetition shapes culture.

Multiplying H.E.A.R.T.

True leadership isn't defined by what you build alone. It's defined by what you make possible for others—the growth you spark, the courage you cultivate, and the example you set through your own willingness to evolve.

When you lead with H.E.A.R.T.:

- You don't just shape strategy.
- You shape people.
- You shape possibility.
- You create environments where others feel safe to grow, stretch, and reimagine who they can become.

But the ripple begins with you.

Cultures don't rise because leaders are perfect.

They rise because leaders stay committed to their own evolution—the quiet, steady work of improving how they listen, how they decide, how they show up, and how they lead.

When you keep growing, your team keeps growing.

When you keep learning, your culture keeps learning.

When you evolve, others follow.

That's not just culture.

That's legacy.

That's leading with H.E.A.R.T.

Looking Ahead:
When Leadership Gets Heavy

You've moved the rug. Trusted yourself. Trusted others. Transformed from within.

But the journey isn't over. Because after every transformation, life will test it. There will be days you feel like starting over. Days when courage slips. Moments when the rug you just moved tries to slide back.

That's normal.

In the next chapter, we talk about the quiet perseverance leadership requires—when the pressure builds, when energy wanes, when everything asks more of you than you feel ready to give.

Because leading with H.E.A.R.T. isn't a finish line, it's a lifelong practice.

Let's keep going.

Chapter 7:

Persevere – When the Rug Slips Again

"Courage doesn't always roar. Sometimes it's the quiet voice at
the end of the day saying, 'I will try again tomorrow.'"
—MARY ANNE RADMACHER

Transformation isn't a destination. It's a cycle. And the hardest
part isn't the breakthrough—it's what comes after.

After the Ascent Comes the Endurance

We love the big moments of growth—the keynote, the launch, the
pivot, the plan. But the real work of leadership? It happens in the after.

In the quiet.

In the repetition.

In the choice to show up again, even when the rug you've just moved
tries to slide back under your feet.

You may have picked up this book during a season of disruption—a
moment when your footing felt unsure. Maybe it was burnout, a leadership shift, a personal crossroads, or just a quiet sense that you were
meant for something more.

You started this journey because you were ready to move a rug in your life, even if you didn't have the words for it yet.

Now here you are. You've questioned old beliefs. You've reimagined what's possible. You've dared to lead differently.

And now, the real test begins: Will you keep going?

The Myth of Constant Momentum

We live in a world that glorifies hustle and constant growth. Nonetheless, leadership isn't linear.

Even the strongest leaders hit walls. Even the most visionary plans lose steam. Even the most evolved cultures face setbacks.

What matters is not whether we stumble—it's how we respond when we do.

Do we pause and reflect? Do we ask for help? Do we remember our why?

Or do we hide, pretend, and push through until we burn out?

Real H.E.A.R.T. Powered Leadership™ means acknowledging the dips. The fatigue. The days when you're not okay—and giving yourself (and your team) permission to be human.

A Personal Practice of Resilience

There was a time when I believed resilience meant pushing through no matter what. Keep going. Don't stop. Stay strong.

But true resilience, I've learned, is about knowing when to rest. When to reset. When to rebuild.

It's about noticing the signs:

- When you start numbing out instead of tuning in.
- When the joy fades and only obligation remains.
- When the rug you once moved becomes heavy again.

That's not failure. That's a signal.

And it's an invitation to return to yourself.

Kevin's Take: Repetition Builds Resilience

In the organizations we work with, it's not the most brilliant strategy that sustains growth—it's the repeatable habits. The rituals that reinforce values. The leadership behaviors that stay consistent, even when outcomes don't. Perseverance isn't just personal. It's cultural.

—Kevin G. Ordoñez

The Rug of Perfection Pressure

We often think we have to be "on" all the time. The world only values the confident, polished version of us. That if we admit struggle, we lose credibility.

But the truth? Pretending is exhausting.

The rug in this chapter is perfection.

The belief that strength means always being okay. That leadership means always having the answer. That growth means never needing to pause.

Let's move that rug.

Let's normalize:

- Saying, "I need help."
- Saying, "I need a break."
- Saying, "I don't know—but I'll figure it out."

Rug Reflection:
The Rug of Shared Blind Spots

Not all rugs are personal—some belong to the team. They show up as inherited beliefs, unspoken rules, and cultural habits that no one questions because everyone has learned to work around them. These shared blind spots are the hardest to name, not because they're hidden, but because they feel familiar.

Yet they're often the very rugs that cause a team or organization to slip back into old patterns—even after meaningful progress has been made.

Seeing them isn't about blame. It's about courage. The courage to recognize what's quietly holding the team back and the willingness to move forward together.

Use the following prompts to reflect with your team:

- **What are we assuming that might not be true anymore?**
  Assumptions age faster than strategies.

  _____

  _____

  _____

- **Which values do we talk about—and which ones do we reinforce through our behavior?**
  Culture is lived, not stated.

  _____

  _____

  _____

- **Where are we choosing comfort over clarity or avoiding discomfort in the name of harmony?**
  Avoidance is often the first sign that an old rug has shifted back into place.

  _____

  _____

  _____

- **What conversations are we circling around instead of addressing directly?**
  The longer a truth goes unspoken, the heavier it becomes.

  _____

  _____

  _____

- **What familiar behaviors suggest we're slipping back into patterns we meant to leave behind?**
  Regression is normal—ignoring it is not.

  _____

  _____

  _____

- **What expectations or habits do we still follow simply because "that's how we've always done it"?**
  Unexamined norms often become ceilings.

The Practice:
The Reset Routine

Progress is rarely linear. Even after meaningful transformation, leaders and teams slip back into old patterns. The point of perseverance isn't perfection—it's the willingness to reset quickly and return to what matters.

This practice helps you and your team create a simple, repeatable way to regain clarity when the unexpected happens or when you feel yourself reverting to old habits.

Step 1:
Name the Slip

Ask yourself or your team:
"What rug did we just trip over?"
Don't overanalyze. Don't justify.
Just name the moment honestly.

Step 2:
Identify the Trigger

Reflect:
"What triggered this shift back into the old pattern?"
Fear?
Fatigue?
Pressure?
Ambiguity?
Lack of clarity?
Understanding the trigger prevents future repetition.

Step 3:
Anchor the Truth

Ask:

"What do we know to be true that we temporarily forgot?"

Your HEART commitments.

Your values.

Your new identity.

Your new expectations.

This reinforces alignment without blame.

Step 4:
Choose the Smallest Next Step

Don't try to fix everything at once. Ask:

"What is one step we can take right now to get back on track?"

Perseverance is built through micro-recovery, not massive overhaul.

Step 5:
Recommit

Close with one shared commitment:

"Here's how we'll move forward from here."

Perseverance grows when teams see recovery as part of leadership, not a failure of it.

Micro-Moves:
Persevere With Purpose

These micro-moves help leaders stay grounded when things slip, shake, or get messy—which they always will. Perseverance is not about never stumbling; it's about choosing how you respond when you do.

- **Name one slip without judgment.**
  Awareness creates momentum.

- **Reset expectations for the day—not the month.**
  Shrink the timeframe to regain control.

- **Ask someone you trust for a truth you need to hear.**
  Outside perspective prevents overreaction.

- **Revisit your "New Me" identity line.**
  Transformation strengthens when reinforced.

- **Take a five-minute pause before making a pressured decision.**
  Clarity arrives when urgency loosens.

- **Reinstate a boundary you relaxed without noticing.**
  Most regressions start with a small leak.

- **Have one honest conversation you've been postponing.**
  Avoidance turns small rugs into big ones.

- **Celebrate one example of resilience you demonstrated today.**
  Recognition builds confidence for tomorrow.

- **Ask your team: "What's one thing we need to tighten back up?"**
  Micro-course corrections prevent major drift.

- **Choose progress over perfection—again and again.**
  Perseverance is repetition, not reinvention.

Leading Through the Long Game

The chapters you've lived—Humanize, Empower, Ascend, Reimagine, Transform, Evolve, Persevere—have shaped something remarkable within you.

But here's the truth: they're not steps to finish. They're cycles to live.

You'll return to them again and again—each time life shifts, each time leadership stretches you, each time the rug moves beneath your feet.

Don't fear the repeat. Welcome it.

Because every return means you're rising from a deeper place of wisdom.

And now, you don't just walk the path.

You are the path.

That's how you lead with H.E.A.R.T.

Chapter 8:

Keep Moving the Rug –
Living with H.E.A.R.T.

"Disruption doesn't end when the chapter closes.
In fact, it often begins just after the last page."
— SHERRY WHITAKER BUDZIAK

You've come far.

You've humanized your leadership. You've empowered others. You've ascended through challenges. You've reimagined what's possible. You've transformed from within. You've helped others evolve. You've learned to persevere.

But the truth is—this work never really ends.

Not because you've failed.

Because you're alive.

Because the world keeps shifting, and so do we. Because leadership is not a finish line. It's a commitment to stay present, stay open, and keep moving forward—with H.E.A.R.T.

Living with H.E.A.R.T.

Leading with H.E.A.R.T. is not a checklist to complete or a badge to display. It's a rhythm. A steady way of showing up—for yourself and for others—day after day, meeting after meeting, disruption after disruption. It's how you lead when the systems break, when the feedback is tough, when the path shifts, and when the rug moves… again.

H.E.A.R.T. is the compass that guides you back to who you want to be as a leader—and who you want your teams to become alongside you.

Humanize—see yourself and others as human first.
Extend empathy inward, then outward.
Courage begins with compassion.

Empower—trust your own voice and create space for others to use theirs.
Leadership multiplies when control loosens.

Ascend—rise into your next version and lift others as you climb.
No one ascends alone.

Reimagine—challenge your assumptions and encourage your teams to challenge theirs.
Possibility grows when curiosity is shared.

Transform—shift your identity and model evolution so others feel safe to evolve too.
Change takes root when leaders live it.

This framework isn't meant to sit on a shelf.
It's meant to be lived—in you first, then through you.
Use it when momentum fades and you're questioning your next step.
Use it when a teammate loses confidence or a team loses its way.
Use it when the next disruption arrives faster than the last.
Use it when old habits whisper louder than new ones.
Use it when the future feels just a little too uncertain.

H.E.A.R.T. is both an inner compass and a cultural blueprint.

Lead yourself with it.

Lead others with it.

Return to it when you drift, and share it when your team needs direction.

Because the truth is simple:

The rug will move again.

And again.

And again.

But now, you don't just know how to move the rug —you know how to move yourself and others forward with it.

When you lead with H.E.A.R.T., you don't simply survive disruption.

You shape what comes after it—for yourself, for your team, and for the people who follow your lead.

The Real Chain Reaction of H.E.A.R.T.

What starts within you doesn't stay with you. You've already begun the chain reaction. Remind yourself that you are the kind of leader who lifts rugs, opens minds, and makes people feel like they belong at the table.

Someone around you is watching how you lead, how you pause, how you choose courage when it would be easier to retreat. And because of your example, they'll start moving their own rug.

They'll speak up.

They'll reimagine.

They'll rise.

This is the true legacy of leadership—not what you build, but who you help build next.

Kevin's Take: The Legacy We Leave

At the end of every engagement, I always ask: What changed that can't be undone? The answer isn't usually about tech or process. It's mindset. It's culture. It's the belief that people matter, growth is possible, and courage is contagious. That's H.E.A.R.T. in action.

—Kevin G. Ordoñez

The Rug of What Comes Next

The journey doesn't end when you move the rug once. It continues every time you pause, listen, realign, and choose the next right step. These final reflections help you look ahead with honesty and hope—grounded in everything you've learned and everything you're becoming.

Use the prompts below to journal in the space provided:

• **Which part of H.E.A.R.T. is calling to you right now—and why?**
   The whispers often show you where your next growth lives.

_____

_____

_____

• **What rug are you still standing on that you now have the courage to move?**
   Awareness is the starting point. Action is the shift.

_____

_____

_____

• **Where are you ready to begin again—with more grace, more clarity, and more truth?**
   Every reset is an opportunity to rise differently.

_____

_____

_____

The Practice:
Your H.E.A.R.T. Declaration

Take a moment to anchor what you're carrying forward. This declaration is your reminder of who you're becoming —and the leader you choose to be when the rug moves again.

Complete the following sentences:

- **The belief I'm choosing to release is …**

_____

_____

_____

- **The part of my leadership I'm committed to strengthening is …**

_____

_____

_____

- **The ripple I want to create starts with …**

_____

_____

_____

Write it.

Say it out loud.

Place it somewhere visible.

Revisit it whenever you feel yourself slipping into old patterns or when disruption knocks on your door.

Declarations don't change you —

Your commitment to them does.

Micro-Moves:
Live H.E.A.R.T. Today

You don't need sweeping change to sustain momentum.
You need one small act of intention—repeated over time.
Choose one micro-move today:

- **Send a genuine thank-you note.**
  Recognition shifts culture.

- **Ask a bold, honest question.**
  Curiosity opens possibility.

- **Delegate with trust instead of control.**
  Empowerment grows capacity.

- **Celebrate someone's progress—including your own.**
  What you notice multiplies.

- **Rest when you're tired.**
  Sustainable leadership requires a sustainable leader.

Small moves.
Steady moves.
Moves that create big ripples.

Your Next Chapter Begins Now

If this book meets you in a moment of change, uncertainty, or quiet frustration, I hope it reminds you of YOUR power. If it found you in a season of growth, I hope it gave you language for what you're building.

Wherever it finds you, I hope you leave knowing this:

- You don't need to wait to be ready.
- You don't need to know the entire path.
- You just need to move the rug that's in front of you—and trust that the next step will appear.

That's how you lead with H.E.A.R.T.

Let's keep going.

Want to Take This Further?

If you're wondering how H.E.A.R.T. shows up in your leadership and across your entire organization, our team at .orgSource (www.orgsource. com) developed the *Future Readiness Assessment* for that exact reason. It's a practical tool that helps teams reflect on their culture, adaptability, digital maturity, and leadership alignment. Whether you're a CEO or an emerging leader, this assessment creates space to ask: *Are we ready for what's next?* And more importantly: *How can we lead it—with H.E.A.R.T.?*

Epilogue:

The Rug Revolution

When we first started writing this book, we thought we were offering a framework—a guide to navigating change with more humanity, more trust, more courage.

But somewhere along the way, it became something bigger. It became a revolution.

Not the loud kind with banners or headlines—the quiet kind that begins inside one person at a time.

It begins the moment a leader pauses long enough to notice the invisible rug everyone's tripping over—and chooses to move it.

It begins when someone decides that survival isn't enough, that it's time to rise.

It begins when a team reimagines an old system, when an individual releases an outdated belief, when a community redefines what it means to belong.

The rug metaphor may sound simple, but moving the rug is never just about the rug. It's about interrupting patterns that no longer serve us. It's about choosing growth over fear—again and again.

And ultimately, it's about becoming the kind of leader—and the kind of human—who makes it safe for others to grow too.

The Invitation

This book isn't the end.

It's your beginning.

Move one rug today—literally or metaphorically.

Name what others are too tired to name.

Start the conversation others keep avoiding.

Every rug you move, every space you clear, every belief you update becomes a foundation someone else can stand on. Your courage creates a ripple effect you may never fully see.

But trust this:

It matters.

You matter.

How you lead matters.

The Rug Revolution is already happening—one moved rug at a time.

And you are part of it.

Let's go move the world.

With H.E.A.R.T.

If you've made it this far, you are already part of the *Rug Revolution*.

You are someone willing to question what others have accepted.

You are someone willing to sit in the tension of change.

You are someone willing to rise—not once, but again and again.

You don't have to lead perfectly.

You just have to lead with truth.

With presence.

With H.E.A.R.T.

H.E.A.R.T. is not a tactic.

It's a way of moving through the world:

Humanize—See the person first, including yourself.

Empower—Create the conditions for others to grow.

Ascend—Step into your voice and invite others to step into theirs.

Reimagine—Refuse to accept routine as destiny.

Transform—Become the leader your next chapter requires.

This is not a one-time shift.

It is a lifetime practice—a rhythm you return to when the rug steadies and when it slips, when the path is clear and when it fractures beneath your feet.

You now know how to name the rugs.

You now know how to move them.

And more importantly, you know how to help others move theirs.

Leadership is not defined by how rarely you fall.

Leadership is defined by how willingly you rise —

and how many people rise because you did.

As you step forward, carry H.E.A.R.T. with you.

Let it guide your choices, your conversations, your culture, and your courage.

The rug will move again.

But now you won't fear the shift.

You'll lead through it.

May you always have the courage to see the rug,

the strength to move it,

and the heart to help others move theirs.

Move the Rug Manifesto

I will notice the rugs I've been tripping over.
I will name what needs to change—with honesty and without apology.
I will move the rug, even when it's uncomfortable.
I will choose growth over familiarity.
I will choose truth over ease.
I will choose courage over silence.
I will lead with H.E.A.R.T.:

- Humanize—I will see myself and others with compassion.
- Empower—I will trust first and create space for others to rise.
- Ascend—I will step into my voice and help others find theirs.
- Reimagine—I will question what no longer serves.
- Transform—I will become the leader my next chapter requires.

I will not wait for permission.
I will not shrink to make others comfortable.
I will not pretend it's fine when it isn't.
I will lead forward—with clarity, with courage, and with the strength I already carry.
The rug is not the story.
How I move it is.

(Sign your name here. Make it real.)

Continue the Journey

This book is just the beginning.

If these ideas resonated with you—if you're ready to stop tripping over old beliefs and start leading with H.E.A.R.T.—we invite you to go deeper.

.orgSource can provide you with a series of experiences and tools to help you and your team move from insight to action. Visit www.orgsource.com to learn more.

Executive Coaching

Personalized leadership support to help you navigate disruption, gain clarity, and lead with confidence.

Workshops & Retreats

Immersive, hands-on sessions for boards, teams, and full organizations looking to build culture, capacity, and connection.

The .orgSource H.E.A.R.T. Powered Leadership™ Newsletter

Monthly insights, case studies, and tools to keep your leadership sharp and your thinking fresh.

Join the Movement:

Tag your story with *#MovetheRug* on LinkedIn or Instagram.

Share how you're leading differently. Inspire someone else to move their rug too.

Ready to lead forward?

Discover resources, tools, and inspiration for your leadership journey. Plus learn more about *Jules Moves the Rug,* a children's book that brings these lessons to young readers.

Visit www.rugthebook.com or scan the QR code.

You don't have to lead alone.
We're here to walk with you—step by step, rug by rug.

THE *RUG* ISN'T THE STORY.
HOW YOU MOVE IT IS.